70x7

A Christian Perspective on Forgiveness

Susan Pryor

70 x 7
A Christian Perspective on Forgiveness

by Susan Pryor

ISBN:978-1-935018-89-6

Edited by: Megan Tasdeler
Interior Design: Leo Ward
Cover Design: Aydin Tasdeler

PUBLISHED BY:
Five Stones Publishing
A DIVISION OF:
The International Localization Network
randy2905@gmail.com
ILNcenter.com

DEDICATION

To Jesus

It is through Your sacrifice on the cross that we have the gifts of forgiveness—and of forgiving.

TABLE OF CONTENTS

INTRODUCTION ONE

We are part of a society that is living on the edge. First, we are on the border that indicates that life as we know it is drastically and permanently changing. Further, we are on the verge of Satan's greatest offensive of aggressive terror against the saints of God. Finally, we are on the boundary of a much greater dimension of the power of God that will culminate in the return of His Son, Jesus Christ. In other words, we are on the dividing line between what has been and what will be.

This precarious position on the edge of both chaos and glory means living in turmoil. There is a certain tension in knowing that our position on the brink presents us with three options:

1. Give in to and be ruled by the enemy, Satan, until we are indistinguishable from the world he dominates.

2. Give in to our carnal nature and live within its fleshly, unholy parameters.

3. Give in to God and be as He is and do as He wants us to do.

In narrowing the general down to the particular, one area many of us now find ourselves in turmoil about involves forgiveness. More and more of us are being brought to the place that demands that we make decisions about forgiveness. Within this specific sphere we have the same three options:

1. Follow the example of Satan who never forgives, who leads us into unforgiveness, and who uses our sin of unforgiveness as the legal basis for establishing his authority over unforgiven areas of our lives.

2. Follow the way of the world, either by letting self-pity and resentment of what we have suffered at the hands of others to send down a deep root of bitterness or by allowing denial and lack of accountability to produce an unforgiving heart.

3. Emulate and imitate God who, in spite of all insult and offense, freely forgives both offense and offenders.

No past moment of life has ever been outside the blessing of His forgiveness. No present second of being is independent of His gift of forgiveness. No future will take place without the assurance of His on-going forgiveness.

In the past when we were unbelievers, our salvation depended on and waited for our personal understanding of the message of the cross: that provision for the forgiveness of our sins had been made through the blood of Jesus Christ. As each of us individually availed ourselves of that provision, as we confessed our sins and asked Him to forgive them and to become our Savior, we were forgiven (Acts 10:43). In the present, one way we can walk out our salvation is by extending His forgiveness to others. Surely in the future, our hope of heaven or of eternity in the presence of God is a reality only because a forgiving Lamb and a forgiven and forgiving lamb have become one.

If our lives are a journey that extend from needing forgiveness to being forgiven to walking in forgiveness, and finally to spending eternity among the forgiven, then surely we must learn about forgiveness. Since God is the Author and Source of forgiveness, we are completely dependent on Him to lead the way. Accordingly, we must seek His lordship in our journey over the edge.

Father,

> As life changes, as unknown and sometimes undesirable currents swirl all around us, as events prove uncertain and people unfaithful, we know that You are God. We know that You are the Rock—The Faithful and True One, The Everlasting Father whose perfect love is always extended toward us. It is You, Father, who sent Your Son Jesus to die so that through His sacrifice, provision was made for the forgiveness of our sins. When He arose from death, you *"made this Jesus ... both Lord and Christ"* (Acts 2:36 NKJV).

Jesus, You are Lord of all. Therefore, You are Lord of forgiveness. You are our model and example. As we seek to walk in Your footsteps, please extend Your lordship over us. Be Leader as we follow, Ruler as we yield, Governor as we choose, and Victor as we triumph over the enemy of unforgiveness.

Thank You, Father. Thank You, Jesus, Lord and Christ. Help us, Holy Spirit.

Now, with God on our side, when our calm is shattered, when offense comes, when we are wounded and bruised by some who are unaware they've harmed us or crushed by those whose offense has been deliberate, we can yet be obedient to God and forgive. Our path from forgiven to forgiving may involve ignorance, denial, lack of accountability, pride, and even a certain amount of reluctance. Yet as we journey, if we will allow God to change our hearts, the secret, self-centered, hesitant question that lies deep within us can change from "Why should I forgive?" to "Why must I forgive?" And as the journey continues, the searching question, "Why must I forgive?" can yield to a heartfelt query, "Lord, how can I forgive?"

Hopefully this book will help to answer those questions.

PART 1

THE BASICS OF FORGIVENESS

Chapter 1

FORGIVENESS IS.....

Years ago, many of us were privileged to read a little book named, *Happiness is.....* by Charles Shultz. Its contents featured the delightful wisdom of a Peanuts character named Charlie Brown. Shultz finished the book title's opening statement in a variety of colorful and descriptive ways, all of which defined some aspect of happiness.

Though we are concerned with a different topic, perhaps an adaption of the same line will again provoke us into personal stretching. Perhaps we will begin to see that a study of forgiveness might include a variety of things we had not considered before, yet all of which add to our understanding.

If we are to discover what forgiveness is, we must arrive at a working definition. According to *Funk and Wagnall's Dictionary*, forgiveness is:

- to extend mercy
- to grant pardon
- to release from obligation toward

- to cease to demand penalty concerning
- to cease to blame
- to cease to feel resentment toward or hold anything against another
- to grant freedom

What *Funk and Wagnall's Dictionary* didn't state is that forgiveness is God's eternal love in action.

Chapter 2

THE FOUNT OF SIN

An appropriate place to begin a book about forgiveness is with an explanation of the need of forgiveness.

INHERENT SIN

Long, long ago God embarked on an ambitious plan: creation. Sovereignly, over a course of time, He spoke forth powerful words commanding forth light; the firmament or Heaven; the earth, grasses and trees; the sun, moon, and stars; and living creatures in the sea, in the sky, and on the earth. Finally, as the zenith of His labor of love, God created man.

This man, formed from the dust of the ground, was created in the image of God (Genesis 1:26). He was a spirit being in direct contact and intimate relationship with God by the Holy Spirit.

This man was placed in a perfect home: the Garden of Eden. His purpose was to worship the God who created him and to administer His kingdom on earth first by extension: *"Be fruitful and multiply; fill the earth...."* (Genesis 1:28 NKJV) and second, by dominion: "….*have dominion over … every living thing that moves on the earth*" (Genesis 1:28 NKJV). God's only stipulation to the man, Adam, was that he was not to eat from the tree of the knowledge of good and evil that was in the garden. His solemn warning should His command be ignored was very pointed: "….*for in the day that you eat of it you shall surely die*" (Genesis 2:17 NKJV).

Sadly, this idyllic setting and this intimate relationship with God did not last. Satan, who had been thrown out of heaven and down to earth, invaded God's garden. He manipulated and deceived Eve, the woman God formed from Adam's rib. He cunningly suggested that she, who had been formed in God's image and was therefore already like God, could become more like God (Genesis 3:5). The path to such exaltation was to disobey the very One who had formed her by eating that which He had forbidden. Not only did she eat but Adam did also.

In so doing, they brought disaster on themselves and, by extension, on the whole of the human race. In disobeying God, in doing exactly what He had commanded them not to do, they set a series of events in motion. First, they sinned and allowed sin to invade their home and lives. Second, their spirits, created to be in intimate relationship with the Spirit of God, were deadened. As there could be no more spiritual communication between created and Creator, man was now a natural being whose soul and flesh predominated. Third, their eyes were opened. They recognized their nakedness and tried to cover themselves with leaves. Fourth, when God came to talk with them, they hid from Him. Fifth, when God confronted them, they blamed others for their own choices of evil.

Rather than have them eat of the tree of life that was also in the garden and live in their fallen state eternally, God mercifully sent them out of the Garden of Eden. Although they had been created to live forever, in time each of them would die as a foretold consequence of their sin.

Unfortunately for us, their sin did not affect just them. God intended that the offspring of Adam and Eve be born in sinless perfection in the beauty of holiness just as their parents had been. Such was not to be. Adam and Eve were prototypes. They were representatives of the human race. When they sinned, sin nature invaded not only their beings but also those of their offspring. The apostle Paul explains: *"….through one man sin entered the world, and death through sin, and thus death spread to all men"* (Romans 5:12 NKJV). Or, as David recognized, *"I was brought forth in iniquity"* (Psalm 51:5 NKJV).

When Adam and Eve subsequently had children, each one inherited and was therefore born with their parents' sin nature. Each, infected by their parents' sin, entered the world with sin already in him. Further, as the children of Adam and Eve were affected by sin so were the their grandchildren, their great grandchildren, and all successive generations down to the present day. Again Paul explains: *"For all have sinned and fall short of the glory of God"* (Romans 3:23 NKJV). If fallen mankind could not find a way to be forgiven of Adam and Eve's original sin against God, men and women would spend eternity out of the presence of God for, *"The wages of sin is death"* (Romans 6:23 NKJV).

Each individual born into the world has the sin of Adam and Eve inherent in his or her being. Each is responsible to acknowledge that sin, and each must be forgiven of it.

PERSONAL SIN

In addition to inherited sin there is another source of sin in which each person in the world engages. That is personal sin. The apostle John tells us, *"If we say that we have no sin, we deceive ourselves, and the truth is not in us"* (1 John 1:8).

As stated, although Adam and Eve were created in the perfection of innocence as spiritual beings, everybody born into the world after them were not and are not. Everyone in every generation born after Adam and Eve fell reflects the fallen rather than the perfect state of their ancestors. They are soulish beings ruled by wrong thoughts, vain imaginations, misinformation, disinformation, and idle speculations of their fallen minds, the corrupted and inappropriate expression of their fallen passions and emotions, and the unholy expressions of their fallen will. Too, each is a fleshly creature governed by the unholy demands of physical cravings and sensual pleasures.

Far from the bliss of the Garden of Eden, each sins and each is responsible to make things right by acknowledging this sin and seeking a way out of it.

How is this possible? How is original sin erased? How is personal sin forgiven?

Remember, forgiveness is God's eternal love in action.

Chapter 3

WHO IS SINNED AGAINST?

Perhaps a deeper explanation is needed as to why there is all this fuss about sin.

Long ago God fashioned from nothing a whole new world and the creatures that would inhabit that world. As Creator of creation, He was Lord of it. As Originator, He was authorized to rule over it. To do so, He set standards of conduct and rules of government which His creatures, mankind, were to obey.

These norms were known in at least two ways. First, they were born into humans. Mankind was created in the image of God. God's very Being was imprinted into human nature. Therefore, His standards of right and wrong, His principles of acceptable conduct, His nature and character were imbedded into people. The fall of Adam and Eve did not change this fundamental truth.

Second, people knew His divine principles by revelation. In the Old Testament, the issuing forth of the Ten Commandments is the most well known unveiling of God's standards. Through them God declared His criteria of conduct between people as they should relate to God and as they should relate to each other. In the New Testament, the Sermon on the Mount is an example whereby God made known His choices for human conduct. Violation of these standards was and is sin.

In the Old Testament, several words describe sin. One is *hata* or missing the mark. At a deeper level is the word *pesa*, which is rebellion or revolt against the standard. One last description of sin is *awon*. This is iniquity or twisting the standard. In the New Testament, sin is generally called *hamartia*, the missing of the mark set by divine standard. Or it is *adikia*, which is wrongdoing, unrighteousness, or injustice. As the *Encyclopedia of Biblical Words* describes it, "Sin is conscious human action that causes visible harm to other persons in violation of the divine standard."

Note well! Each variation of sin is a violation of divine, not human, standard. Therefore each is a violation or sin against the Creator of that standard—God.

With this brief background, we go on. Long ago Satan, a powerful, created being, resided in heaven with God. Somehow, in that place of perfection, sin entered his heart (Ezekiel: 28:1-19). Not content to serve God, Satan wanted to be like Him. Rather than worship his Creator, he wanted to be worshipped. Listen to his self-adulation, his rebellion, and his dark goals:

I will ascend into heaven,
I will exalt my throne above the stars of God;

I will also sit on the mount of the congregation on the far-
thest sides of the north;
I will ascend above the heights of the clouds,
I will be like the Most High." (Isaiah 14:13-14 NKJV)

Clearly Satan lusted after the rule rightly held by God. He wanted to establish his own self-honoring, evil, violent standards over God's people. To gain his own ends, he rose up in revolt against God. In his treasonous act of aggression he didn't just miss the mark; he smashed divine standards. As a result, God, in righteous judgment, threw him out of heaven and down to earth.

Being out of the presence of God did not dim Satan's blind ambitions. Being in a new location did not change his plan to control creation. Instead, he found a race called humans living on earth. Since he could no longer conduct face-to-face warfare against God, Satan came up with a new plan. He would continue his rebellion against God using the very people God had created in His own image. Men and women would become the vehicle of the working out of his enmity against God.

We know of the tragedy in the Garden of Eden. Through manipulation and lies Satan deceived Eve into sin. She, in turn, influenced Adam to sin. But against whom did they sin? Themselves? No! Satan? No! Though of a different order, he was just a created being as they were. Since both he and they had created nothing and had no authority to establish legal standards or rules for government, both he and they were not sinned against.

It was God whom they sinned against. He had created them. He had given them rules for their relationship with Him and for their service of obedience to Him. It was His mark that was missed. It was His rule that was disobeyed. It was His standard that was rebelled against. It was against God, His nature, His commands to them, and His intention for them that they sinned.

This established a precedent: all sin is against God. Sin may involve people, places, or things, but, at its root, all sin is aimed directly at the heart of God. And through it, Satan still uses men and women to dishonor God.

Can anyone forget David? He sinned by having an adulterous relationship with Bathsheba, he sinned by arranging the death of her husband, and he sinned by not leading his army out to war. Too, as leader and king, David sinned by his bad example before the very people and nation dedicated to God (2 Samuel 11). Crying out to God, his words of confession then might startle us: *"Against **You, You only,** have I sinned, and done this evil in Your sight"* [emphasis added] (Psalm 51:4 NKJV).

In the New Testament, another occurrence shows that sin is against God. It is found in Acts 5. Ananias and Sapphira had sold a possession but kept back part of the proceeds. Their example of pride and greed and their lies and deceit affected the whole of the blossoming Christian community. However, their sin was against God. Peter's specific charge to them is revealing: *"While it remained was it not your own? And after it was sold, was it not in your own control? Why have you conceived this thing in your heart? You have not lied to men **but to God**"* [emphasis added] (Acts 5:4 NKJV).

Make no mistake. What happened to Ananias and Sapphira can happen to anyone. God can speak to people's hearts, but so can Satan. Since the nature and intent of both are total opposites, that leaves mankind in a position of making a choice. We can fill our hearts with Satan's insidious evil and follow him, or we can follow God.

Any who acknowledge that they were born in sin and have committed sin, any who realize that all sin is against God have only one choice. They must go to God, who was sinned against, and ask for His forgiveness. They can and they must, because forgiveness of their sin is God's eternal love in action.

Chapter 4

THE FOUNT OF FORGIVENESS

Forgiveness was unknown in the Garden of Eden. It was unknown because it was unnecessary.

Think for a moment. In Eden, in the beauty, perfection, and holiness of God's sovereign creation, there was no sin and therefore there was no need for forgiveness of sin. The fall of Adam and Eve changed all that.

When our ancestors disobeyed God, they introduced personal sin into their own lives. Though they tried to cover their sin, they quickly found that they could not undo the damage they had done through denial, finger pointing, or self-appointed works. Further, their action introduced sin into the world around them, causing the need for the sin of the world to be forgiven. While Adam and Eve could not provide self-redemption for their sin, God could. And God did.

When Adam and Eve disobeyed God, they brought sin on themselves and, through them, on all their descendants (Romans 5:12). Too, when Adam and Eve sinned and were driven from Eden, they carried sin with them. Where ever they or their descendants went or whatever they did, sin marked their path. Through untold ages and generations the world became a very dark place where people were bereft of spiritual communication with God and where they acted out of their soulish senses or physical lusts. How can the difference be measured between sinful man and the perfect man God created or between the earth now blemished by sin and the perfection of Eden?

Long before the foundation of the world God knew that His created ones would sin. Long before the foundation of the world He had a plan to forgive sin. This plan would quicken humanity from spiritual death into new life and reinstate men and women into right relationship with God through divine sacrifice, blood, and death. Promised in the Garden of Eden (Genesis 3:15), this plan was fulfilled in the Garden of Gethsemane. There, Jesus, God's Son who came to earth to *"save His people from their sins"* (Matthew 1:21 NKJV), became forgiveness.

As years and generations passed and the situation grew even more evil, God worked out this plan to save His creation from sin. It is revealed in the pages of Scripture.

ATONEMENT FOR SIN IN THE OLD COVENANT

According to the Old Covenant law, when a man or a nation sinned, atonement, or an attempt to reconcile relationship with God though sacrifice, had to be made for that sin through precisely proscribed rituals of sacrifice. Different types of sin, different depths of sin (John 19:11), and different reasons for sin each had a temporal remedy through these rituals. In atoning, an innocent animal was brought to a priest and slaughtered. Sin could be covered by means of its shed blood. *"And according to the law almost all things are purified with blood, and without shedding of blood there is no remission"* (Hebrews 9:22 NKJV).

This sacrificial system dealt with sin but it was not the perfect answer for sin. Though it covered sin, it never fully resulted in forgiveness of the sin. *"For it is not possible that the blood of bulls and goats could take away sins"* (Hebrews 10:4 NKJV).

Mercifully, the pages of the Old Testament reveal a more permanent solution. The innocent animal and the shed blood of the Old Covenant sacrifice were types or shadows. All prophesied of the coming of a Savior, an innocent Lamb of God whose shed blood would, once and for all, take away the sin of the world. Rather than just a covering for sin, He would provide true forgiveness.

The prophet Isaiah described the substitutionary sacrifice where God's Lamb took the place of fallen mankind, shed blood for our sin, and provided the means to forgive that sin.

> *Surely He has borne our griefs*
> *And carried our sorrows;*
> *Yet we esteemed Him stricken,*
> *Smitten by God, and afflicted.*
> *But He was wounded for our transgressions,*
> *He was bruised for our iniquities;*
> *The chastisement for our peace was upon Him,*
> *And by His stripes we are healed.*
> *All we like sheep have gone astray;*

We have turned, every one, to his own way;
And the LORD has laid on Him the iniquity of us all.
(Isaiah 53:4-6 NKJV)

FORGIVENESS OF SIN IN THE NEW TESTAMENT

Thousands of years after Isaiah's revelation, timed perfectly according to God's plan, the prophecy was fulfilled. Two thousand years ago, times were evil. The plight of humanity was desperate. The world was drowning, trapped in sin.

Into this foreign and reprobate place God the Father sent God the Son. Jesus gave up the splendors and acclaim of the courts of heaven. Jesus was *"the brightness of His glory and the express image of His person"* (Hebrews 1:3 NKJV), so He could be God's representative on earth. He was miraculously conceived by the Holy Spirit and was born as a Babe to a virgin. As He grew to manhood, He *"increased in wisdom and stature and in favor with God and men"* (Luke 2:52 NKJV). Although living as a Man among men, He remained completely sinless in all He thought, said, or did (2 Corinthians 5:21; Hebrews 4:15).

Two things made Jesus completely different than the men around Him. First, because He was conceived by the Holy Spirit rather than by a natural man, He was born without inherited sin. Second, because He lived a life completely free of sin He remained holy and innocent. Thus, He, and He alone, could meet the Old Testament's condition as an innocent offering. He alone could be the perfect substitute for mankind. He alone was qualified to offer Himself as a substitute to die in our place for our sins. He alone could satisfy the wrath of

God due sin. As a result of this one last perfect sacrifice, we could be forgiven, spiritually reconnected with God, and restored to right relationship with our Father.

Even though He knew the horrific cost, Jesus allowed the sin of mankind to be placed on Him (2 Corinthians 5:21). Though innocent, He suffered and died for the guilty, broken and bleeding on a cross. On a day that outranks all others in human history for infamy, shame, dishonor, wickedness, and majesty, Jesus was taken to a hill called Calvary. There, outside the city, He sacrificed His life for us.

Unlike the on-going Old Testament rite of slaughter, His sacrifice of atonement for sin was so complete that the blood of animals need never be shed again. In fact, His selfless act of love made the bloody rites and rituals concerning atonement outdated and unnecessary.

> So Christ was offered once to bear the sins of many. [emphasis added] (Hebrews 9:28 NKJV)

> Now where there is remission of these, there is no longer an offering for sin. (Hebrews 10:18 NKJV)

Unlike the Old Testament rite that provided limited atonement for personal or national sin, Jesus' sacrifice provided forgiveness for all sin—every single sin that ever has been committed, is being committed, or ever will be committed. John the Baptist recognized this when he said of Jesus, "Behold! The Lamb of God who takes away the sin of the world" (John 1:29 NKJV)!

Unlike the Old Testament rite of animal sacrifice that could only cover sin, Jesus' shed blood brought actual forgiveness for it. Jesus Himself testifies that His blood was shed for the remission of sin: *"Then He took the cup, and gave thanks, and gave it to them, saying, 'Drink from it, all of you. For this is My blood of the new covenant, which is shed for many for the remission of sins'"* (Matthew 26:27-28 NKJV).

His words assured everyone then and assure everyone now that forgiveness is found in the ever-powerful blood of Jesus Christ.

Three days after His death, Jesus, in total triumph over sin, rose from the dead (2 Corinthians 5:15). God honored His suffering and sacrifice for the forgiveness of sin by receiving Him up in glory (1 Timothy 3:16). Jesus, as His name declared, provided all mankind not just with a covering for sin but also with forgiveness of sin. *"Him God has exalted to His right hand to be Prince and Savior, to give repentance to Israel and forgiveness of sins"* (Acts 5:31 NKJV).

Not while mankind was free but when we were slaves to sin, Jesus bled for us. Not while mankind was innocent but when we were guilty, Jesus died for us. Not while mankind was alive in Christ but when we were dead in sin, Jesus gave us new life. Not while mankind was in right relationship with our Creator and Father but when estranged from Him, Jesus provided the means to admit each of us into the family of God. Not while mankind deserved it but when he didn't, Jesus became our Substitute and paid the full price for our sins. In so doing, the love of Jesus made full provision for the full forgiveness of all sin.

That was God's eternal love in action.

How can we say thank You to *"Jesus Christ, the faithful witness, the firstborn from the dead, and the ruler over the kings of the earth. To Him who loved us and washed us from our sins in His own blood"* (Revelation 1:5 NKJV)?

Chapter 5

WHO FORGIVES WHOM?

In a previous chapter, we learned that sin began in the heart of Satan but was loosed into mankind in the Garden of Eden. When Adam and Eve violated holy standards and rejected God's divine rule over them, sin invaded the world. Their sin established the need of forgiveness because God had made His commands and His desires concerning those commands known. Further, their sin established the need for *His* forgiveness because their sin was committed against God. Only God forgives sin.

All three parts of the Godhead are involved in the forgiveness of sin. God the Father knew sin would invade the lives of men. Although the One sinned against, He gave the gift of forgiveness. That gift, Jesus, God's Son, suffered and died in man's place so that sin could be forgiven. God the Holy Spirit is man's guide into that gift.

VERTICAL AND HORIZONTAL FORGIVENESS

When a person has become aware of sin or at last admits that there is sin in his (or her) life, he must go to God, who already knows about that sin, confess that sin, and ask to be forgiven of that sin through the cleansing blood of Jesus Christ. When he does so, he is immediately forgiven and restored to right relationship with God. This man-to-God action is the vertical aspect of forgiveness.

Second, the one who sinned must also go to the individual or group he (or she) harmed by his sin and address the personal side of the problem. He must confess his sin, apologize, and seek to be released from any resentment or ill will his actions have caused. If those who have been betrayed, hurt, or offended respond with grace, the one who caused the problem is released. He may or may not be restored to personal relationship. This person-to-person action is the horizontal aspect of forgiveness.

Stated another way, when asked to do so, God is ever gracious to forgive **sin**. When asked to do so, we must release or give up all resentment toward the sinner.

FORGIVING SIN

Our Bibles prove the truth of the statement that because all sin is against God, only God can and will forgive sin.

Forgiveness in the Old Covenant:

Many years after the events of the Garden of Eden, a famine rose that enveloped the land. Many people groups, including the Hebrews, suffered because of it. Some of those Hebrews in desperate need of food were the sons of Jacob.

In nearby Egypt there was a man named Joseph who was an extraordinary overseer of the land. He had not only foreseen and forewarned Pharaoh of the famine, but he also stockpiled an abundance of grain in advance of the famine to have provision for the Egyptians through it.

Years earlier this Joseph, who was himself a Hebrew, had been sold as a slave and taken against his will to Egypt by the perverse deeds of his blindly jealous brothers. There, through the passage of time, he overcame rejection, lies, betrayal, imprisonment, and a host of other evils to rise to his position of prominence. He was second only to Pharaoh in governing the land.

When the starving sons of Jacob arrived in Egypt to seek food, Joseph recognized them as the very brothers who had betrayed him. He called them into his presence and, with tears and deeply felt emotion, he revealed his identity to them. Their joy in their reunion quickly led to fear of retribution for their past actions. They finally admitted their sins and asked Joseph to *"forgive the trespass of your brothers and their sin for they did evil to you"* (Genesis 50:17 NKJV). Joseph's reply came from a deep well of wisdom: *"Do not be afraid, for am I **in the place of God?"** [emphasis added] (Genesis 50:19 NKJV).

In essence, Joseph declared that he could not forgive their sin. Only God could. He did, however, forgive them. Joseph, whose whole life had been upended and who had suffered through years of torture and torment, found it in his heart to assure his brothers: *"Now therefore, do not be afraid. I will provide for and support you and your little ones. And he comforted them [imparting cheer, hope, strength] and spoke to their hearts [kindly]"* (Genesis 50:21 AMP).

In the books of the prophets there is a further confirmation that reveals that it is God only who can forgive sin. Through Isaiah, it is the LORD Himself who declares: *"**I, even**

I, am He who blots out your transgressions for My own sake; And I will not remember your sins" [emphasis added] (Isaiah 43:25 NKJV).

Forgiveness in the New Covenant:

The New Testament confirms the good news that only God forgives sin. One story from its pages makes this truth very clear.

When Jesus was in Capernaum, He met with people to preach the Word to them. So great was His renown, so treasured was His presence that one house in which He taught was filled to capacity with eager listeners. That didn't deter some strong-hearted men on a mission of mercy from trying to reach Him.

When four of them carrying a paralyzed man on a heavy pallet were barred from entry at the door of the house, they somehow hoisted the invalid onto the roof, opened a hole in the roof, and lowered him down through the hole into the presence of Jesus. Touched by this and seeing their faith, Jesus stopped teaching and turned to the paralyzed man and said, *"Son, your sins are forgiven you"* (Mark 2:5 NKJV).

However, Jesus wasn't the only One in whose presence the paralytic found himself. In the crowd filling the house were scribes or experts in the law. Rather than being awed by Jesus' declaration of authority that the man's sins were forgiven, they challenged His words. *"Why does this Man speak blasphemies like this? **Who can forgive sins but God alone?"*** [emphasis added] (Mark 2:7 NKJV).

The scribes were right in recognizing that only God could forgive sin. However, they were wrong in not recognizing that Jesus was God. In response, Jesus challenged His challengers. *"Which is easier, to say to the paralytic, 'Your sins are forgiven you,' or to say, 'Arise, take up your bed and walk?' But that you may know that the Son of Man has power on earth to forgive sins"*—He said to the paralytic, *"I say to you, arise, take up your bed, and go to your house"* (Mark 2:10-11 NKJV).

By His words Jesus was saying, "You say only God can forgive sins? You are right! I am that God!" Demonstrating that revelation in majesty and power, He forgave the man of his sins and miraculously healed him of his paralysis.

None of us are asked to or are able to forgive sin. We have not lived sinless lives. Only Jesus has. We have not shed our blood for the cleansing from sin. Only Jesus has. We have not given our lives to redeem humanity from sin. Only Jesus has. Therefore we are not eligible to deal with sin. Only Jesus is.

FORGIVING THE SINNER

As stated in Chapter 3, all sin is committed against God. However, it is all too often true that sin against God is aimed at people. It is a rare occasion when a person's words, actions, or behaviors do not affect others. Whether involving another individual or including a whole group, such as family, friends, co-workers, or a Christian body, when a person sins he or she hurts, wounds, or offends others by that sin.

Roget's Thesaurus defines offense as "displeasure caused by an insult or slight." If the person targeted by the sin or the one affected by the sin reacts to it by feelings of hurt, anger, resentment, or desire for revenge, he or she has taken offense. Both the one who sinned and the one who has taken offense to personal attack have issues and must seek or extend forgiveness.

Just as things have to be made right with God, so also when anyone sins things must be made right with people. While the offended ones cannot forgive the sin, they can forgive the person who sinned.

Jesus explained this to His disciples in Luke 17:3 (NKJV): *"Take heed to yourselves. If your brother sins against you, rebuke him; and if he repents, forgive **him**"* [emphasis added].

Note well. Scripture does not say we are to forgive our brother's sins. We are to forgive *him.*

When we are hurt by another, we must forgive the one who sinned against us. No one said it was going to be easy, but no matter how deep the wound, how grievous the betrayal, how outrageous the action, we must forgive. We must refuse to hold any resentment or ill will, and we must release the errant one from any future debt or obligation concerning his actions.

Sometimes, when the pain is so great, forgiveness seems impossible. At these times, it is well to remember the depth of the mercy of God's forgiveness towards us, and, by this, to gain the intention and strength to extend His blessing to the one who caused us pain.

THE LORD'S PRAYER

All of this is summed up in two of the most well known verses in the Bible. In the Lord's Prayer, the difference between vertical and horizontal forgiveness or the difference between forgiving the sin or the sinner is made clear.

Jesus had begun His public ministry by preaching, teaching, healing, and delivering many (Matthew 4). When great multitudes were following Him, He went to a mountain, sat down, gathered His disciples, and began to speak. He revealed those lovely words of blessing that are called the Beatitudes. He declared several changes that had to be made in the lives of those who followed Him. When he compared *"You have heard it said"* with *"but I say to you,"* He was rejecting Pharisaic interpretation of the Law, oral tradition, and the old man (Matthew 5).

Then, in the wilderness with multitudes in attendance, Jesus declared the way to communicate with God. Specifically rebuking Pharisaic hypocrisy as the only or right way to live, He taught on prayer. And, in the midst of teaching His followers how to pray, he instructed on forgiveness.

The Lord's Prayer, rich and beautiful when spoken or sung, was given as a general instruction concerning topics that Christians should include when communing with God. In giving His disciples an example to follow, He opened His prayer by addressing and worshipping His Father. After petitions for His kingdom and for provision, Jesus honed in on the topic of forgiveness with the words *"forgive us our debts"* (Matthew 6:12 NKJV).

According to *Vine's Expository Dictionary of Biblical Words*, the word Jesus used for "debts" is *opheilema*. It means "an expression of that which is legitimately due" or, metaphorically, "of sin as a 'debt' because it demands expiation and thus payment by way of punishment." In other words, Jesus was saying to those who would listen that sin is a type of spiritual debt and that the debt must be discharged spiritually through forgiveness *from God*.

Then, while still addressing His Father, the next phrase of the petition changes from the vertical to the horizontal. As our petition is for forgiveness, so also our promise is to forgive: "*....as we forgive our debtors*" (Matthew 6:12 NKJV).

Again, according to *Vine's*, the word Jesus used for "debtors" is *opheiletes*. It means, "one who owes anything to another" or metaphorically, it is a reference to "those who have not yet made amends to those whom they have injured."

DEBTORS: To differentiate, debtors are people. They are those who have failed in their duty toward us. If the lapse involves money or material things, debtors are those who owe, are delinquent in paying what they owe and who have broken their word or failed to keep promise of repayment. If the failure involves sin, debtors are those who owe and are slow or unwilling to make their offenses and transgressions right.

DEBTS: Debts are what debtors have or create. Spiritually speaking, they are sins and offenses.

We are to forgive our debtors, not their debts. We are to release sinners, not their sins. We are to free offenders, not their offenses.

With His careful choice of words Jesus is teaching that forgiveness requires two actions. The first is a petition to God to forgive our sin; the second is a promise that we will forgive those who have sinned against us.

Confusing these roles leads to problems. For instance, sometimes we are reluctant to forgive if we think that forgiveness is synonymous with asking our Father to condone or to tolerate sin or to permit further ill treatment. Often it is difficult to forgive if we feel that by forgiving, sin is being disregarded and ignored or that the offender will not be held accountable. We may wait a long time to forgive if we believe that we should not do so until the offender is aware of and sorry for his or her sin, confesses it, and asks us for forgiveness first.

Can we see the error in this thinking? In every case, the focus is on the sin and not on the sinner. We are concentrating on the debt and not on the debtor. We are trying to deal with the offense and not the offender. The focus is on hurt feelings (hurt, anger, desire for revenge, or bitterness), and the energy is expended on holding on to these feelings in order to punish the debtor or to make him or her feel pain too.

God has a different will, word, and way. He asks us to rise above internal objections and walk worthily as new creations. We are commanded to deny carnal attitudes and worldly reactions and, as He would, to forgive our debtors. Through Him, we are asked and are able to extend our forgiveness to those who have sinned against us. *"And be kind to one another, tender-hearted, forgiving one another, even as God in Christ forgave you"* (Ephesians 4:32 NKJV).

Chapter 6

WHAT SINS ARE FORGIVEN?

So far we have learned that Adam and Eve disobeyed God and in so doing unleashed a root of evil that engulfed the world, that all sin is committed against God, that the fount or source of forgiveness for sin is through the blood shed by Jesus Christ at the cross, and that God alone can forgive sin.

If God has the authority to forgive sin, has provided the means to forgive sin, and longs to forgive sin, the questions might now be asked: What sin does God forgive? Does He forgive just the effects of the original sin committed in Eden or does His mercy and forgiveness also include the personal sins committed in daily life?

Blessedly, the answer is both. Through the sacrifice of Jesus Christ, God can and will forgive the sin inherent in mankind as a result of the fall of Adam and Eve. This forgiveness is called salvation from sin or being born again. After this initial transaction is completed, He can and will forgive the personal sins committed by men and women.

FORGIVENESS OF ORIGINAL OR INHERITED SIN

As is known, when the first man and woman sinned, their sin affected more than just themselves. As a result of their disobedience to a direct command of God, sin entered their nature. After the fall, when they had children, this sin nature was passed from them to their offspring and from their off-spring into the human race. Every man or woman in every succeeding generation down to the present day was and is born with this sin nature already inherent or within them.

Other disastrous effects of the fall are:

- Men and women's spirits were deadened, which caused spirit-to-Spirit communion with God to cease.
- Men and women were dominated by sin nature instead of holiness.
- Men and women became natural beings living by the demands of soul or flesh.
- Men and women were separated from God or were out of relationship with Him.
- Mankind's home was the kingdom of darkness.

Forgiveness of original sin comes courtesy of the finished work of the cross. When Jesus died on the cross, He provided a way to reverse the horrendous results of inherited sin and to restore things to creative order. So great, so miraculous, so all encompassing, so far reaching was His act of love that provision was made available for the forgiveness of all the inherent sin of all people throughout all of time.

During the course of his life, when a man realizes that there is a God but that he isn't close to Him, that the life he lived through his mind, emotions, self-will, or flesh isn't a portrait of holiness, or that his on-going attempts to become a better person continuously fail, he may begin to ponder. Or, when a woman has spent a lifetime doing good works to try to earn entry to heaven but suspects that even her best efforts will never guarantee such a blessing, she may begin to ask questions. When both realize that self-importance, being a "good" person, and doing nice things isn't enough to spend eternity in the presence of God, they have to wonder, what is? If life can only be improved by being rid of the inherited sin that dominates a person's life and disrupts his or her soul, how is sin eradicated? If the desire for a different way of living doesn't match the reality of a life free of the guilt and shame of sin, what is lacking?

The answer is forgiveness.

In shedding His blood, Jesus paid the wages of sin: death (Roman 6:23). In rising from death, He brought new life. Anyone who comes to Him with a sincerely contrite heart and asks for forgiveness for inherited sin is instantly and totally forgiven of that sin and is given the gift of new life.

The blessings don't stop there.

- Men and women's once deadened human spirits are quickened so they are again in direct communication with God's Spirit.
- Men and women's spirits rise to rule over their soul and flesh so they are no longer dominated by senses and impulses.
- Men and women are brought into right relationship with God. In fact, they are adopted into the family of God (John 1:12).

- Men and women's sin natures no longer dominate their beings; they inherit God's divine nature (1 Peter 1:3-4).
- Satan is no longer the master of these men and women; Jesus is both their Savior and their Lord.
- Rather than living in darkness and shadows, men and women are translated into the kingdom of light (1 Peter 2:9).

In short, men and women are released of the guilt and shame of sin and stand in innocence before their Creator, God.

While provision was made two thousand years ago for humanity's release from inherited sin, there is a path that must be followed to activate the provision.

1. When any man or woman realizes something is missing in life and acknowledges that the problem is sin, each must understand that as long as that sin remains, it is a barrier to having a relationship with God. Should any die while that sin stands, he or she would spend not a mere lifetime but an eternity out of the presence of God.

2. He or she must understand and then acknowledge that the only way to be rid of inherited sin is through Jesus Christ. He Himself proclaimed: *"I am the way, the truth, and the life. No one comes to the Father except through Me"* (John 14:6).

3. When anyone comes to Him and asks for forgiveness of inherited sin, he or she is immediately forgiven of that sin. There are no works to perform and no penance to do. It is accomplished by faith in the finished work of the cross.

4. Salvation or being born again is truly a death-to-life experience. By it, all who are dead in sin can receive rich, new life in Christ.

In other words, this salvation experience is mankind's entry into the kingdom of God. By it, inherited sin is removed. Men and women are miraculously and gloriously forgiven of all sin committed up to the moment of their salvation. They are fully freed from all consequences due for their sin; there is no punishment due for it or penalty to pay for it. They are released from all guilt and shame. And no sin committed during the rest of their lives will cause them to come under condemnation for original sin or cause its penalty, death, to be re-imposed. God will never bring up this sin again because it is totally cleansed and removed.

The Bible is quite descriptive of original sin:

> I, even I, am He who blots out your transgressions for My own sake; And I will not remember your sins. (Isaiah 43:25 NKJV)

> No more shall every man teach his neighbor, and every man his brother, saying "know the LORD" for they all shall know Me, from the least of them to the greatest of them, says the LORD. For I will forgive their iniquity, and their sin I will remember no more. (Jeremiah 31:34 NKJV)

> Behold! The Lamb of God who talks away the sin of the world! (John 1:29 NKJV)

> There is therefore now no condemnation to those who are in Christ Jesus, who do not walk according to the flesh, but according to the Spirit. For the law

of the Spirit of life in Christ Jesus has made me free from the law of sin and death. (Romans 8:1-2 NKJV)

If anyone is in Christ, he is a new creation; old things have passed away; behold, all things have become new. (2 Corinthians 5:17 NKJV)

Is there any who would even now let the fount of forgiveness flow? Are there those who desire to be cleansed and forgiven of inherent sin and restored to right relationship with Father God?

Father,

You are gracious and Almighty God. I come to You in my need. There is sin in my soul and flesh. It rules—even dominates—me. With it, in it, I am lost.
Against You only have I sinned. You only can save me from this sin.
I confess my sin to you.
Please forgive me through the blood of Your Son, Jesus.
Thank You, Father.
I receive Your forgiveness.

FORGIVENESS OF PERSONAL SIN

The initial release of original sin is called salvation. Glorious as it is, it is not all there is to it. The Bible declares that after being released from original sin, each must go on to *"work out your own salvation with fear and trembling"* (Philippians 2:12 NKJV). This working out process is called sanctification.

Jesus is the only Man who lived on earth who never sinned. None alive today is Jesus. Therefore, although freed from the guilt of inherited sin and no longer an unwilling slave to the sin nature that once dominated life before salvation, each person still sins. Maybe out of ignorance of the Word, will, and ways of God, maybe while in process of dealing with a besetting sin or changing an old habit, or maybe through a momentary lapse of judgment, each sins.

If we say that we have no sin, we deceive ourselves, and the truth is not in us. (1 John 1:8 NKJV)

If we say that we have not sinned, we make Him a liar, and His word is not in us. (1 John 1:10 NKJV)

Note well! This lapse does not make a new saint a sinner who is in need of salvation again. Salvation, a one-time-only transaction with God, is already complete. However, this lapse does make him or her a child of God who, in weakness, transgressed.

This new sin, though divinely included in Jesus' victory over all sin at the cross, doesn't just go away. It must be dealt with. Just as the person *in sin* once approached God to appropriate forgiveness of original sin, so now the person *who sinned* must come before God to appropriate forgiveness of personal sin. If he does not, the sin becomes a barrier. This barrier is not in his *right relationship* with God that was established through salvation, but in his *intimate relationship* with Him in the on-going process of sanctification.

As Jesus is the propitiation of the sin of the world, so He is also the propitiation for personal sin. The sacrifice of Jesus Christ that was the means of forgiveness of inherited sin is the same means of forgiveness of subsequent personal sin. *"And He Himself is the propitiation for our sins, and not for ours only but also for the whole world"* (1 John 2:2 NKJV).

When a child does something wrong he must go to his father to seek forgiveness. Once forgiven, if he errs in the same way again and again, he must go to his father and be accountable for his actions each time he is disobedient. He must admit what he did and ask for forgiveness. Even if there is a disciplinary action that results from his disobedience, in his going to his father, admitting his fault, and asking to be forgiven, his father will yet confirm his forgiveness.

In the kingdom of God, just as there was a path to forgiveness of inherited sin, so also there are steps to take for a person to receive forgiveness of personal sin.

1. We must repent or change our minds about the appropriateness of a specific work, thought, deed, or attitude.

2. We must confess our sin or agree with God that we have violated the character, nature, name, Word, or will of God by our deed.

3. We must ask for forgiveness of specific sin.

4. Through faith in the eternal, on-going power of the cross we can accept forgiveness from God. *"If we confess our sins, He is faithful and just to forgive us our sins and to cleanse us from all unrighteousness"* (1 John 1:9 NKJV).

5. We can end our cleansing process with heartfelt thanks for God's continuous expressions of love and mercy.

Is there any who sees forgiveness of personal sin in a greater light? Is there any who would even now desire to be cleansed of such sin against God and be restored to closer relationship with Him?

Father,

You are a good and holy God.

You are merciful and ever forgiving.

I am in need of Your forgiveness.

I see that my choice of words (acts, thoughts, attitudes, etcetera) was wrong. It in no way honored You. I am determined not to repeat it.

I confess my sin of _____ to You.

Please forgive me.

I believe that through the blood of Jesus I am cleansed and made whole.

Thank You, Father.

Chapter 7

LAUNCHING PAD

If we are going to be pursuing the knowledge and the practice of forgiveness, there are some fundamental principles that must be understood from the outset.

First, in spite of biblical command to do so, not everyone walks on this path. Perhaps because of denial or immaturity, perhaps because the wounding is so great that some feel time is needed to deal with the pain of betrayal or anger, perhaps because we don't see the potential for personal devastation in the future if we don't deal with the present. For whatever reason, there are those who will not make this journey.

When offense happens there are two human parties involved: the offended and the offender. Often both will know when a problem has sprung up that has begun to hinder their relationship and both will agree that it needs to be dealt with. Accordingly, both will take time or make time to do all that is necessary to set the situation right.

Sometimes though, when an offense has been committed, it is seen through only one pair of (human) eyes. Usually it is the offended who is very public about the situation while the offender either does not see that there is a problem or thinks it is "no big deal." Less often, it is the offender who reveals an offense that the offended may either be unaware of or is in denial about. Thus the situation exists that one declares that there is a problem and the other denies both the problem and any responsibility or accountability concerning it. One is willing to work it out to the point of forgiveness; the other is refusing to.

However, in any situation involving forgiveness, neither side can sit back and wait for the other to make the first move toward peace. Whether offended or offender, both are required to take action. Whether offended or offender, both are commanded to initiate the process of forgiveness.

Concerning the offended: *"Moreover if your brother sins against you, go and tell him his fault between you and him alone. If he hears you, you have gained your brother"* (Matthew 18:15 NKJV).

When wounding has occurred, it is the responsibility of the one who has been hurt to go to his (or her) brother (or sister, friend, co-worker, neighbor, spouse, etcetera). If he allows pride or anger to prevent his going, he sins against God. Whether the offender is unaware of his actions and so doesn't know there is need of a meeting or whether he is all too aware of his offense and is avoiding a confrontation, to not go to the one to whom he has caused offense is sin against that brother.

Concerning the offender: *"Therefore if you bring your gift to the altar, and there remember that your brother has some-*

thing against you, leave your gift there before the altar, and go your way. First be reconciled to your brother, and then come and offer your gift" (Matthew 5:23-24 NKJV).

Whether a person has truly offended another or whether only the one taking offense only perceives and therefore believes that he (or she) has, a situation exists that only the offender can deal with. As soon as he realizes that another has something against him, he must go to his brother. The one being blamed for giving offense must face his accuser. If instead he chooses to laugh it off, to refuse confrontation, or to sarcastically tell the offended to "Get over it!", it is sin against God and further offense against his brother.

This also may be where denial kicks in. If the offender denies that wounding has happened, then he (or she) feels no need to face his accuser. Similarly, if the offended denies that wounding has happened, he (or she) feels no need to bring the offender to accountability. If there is no need of accountability, there is no need to go to one another. And if no one goes, the process of forgiveness is thwarted. Oh, the lack of love in the hearts of those who will not approach their brothers and sisters to release them into the freedom of their forgiveness!

In any case, there should be no waiting for the other to give in and go first. The one to initiate the forgiveness process is the one who realizes the problem exists. Scripture doesn't say to sit in stubborn silence or pained pride and wait to see who will give in first. Rather, Scripture says to both: "Go."

Additionally, forgiveness is not a legalistic formula. It is neither "I'm sorry" quickly and insincerely mumbled under the breath nor a very public, attention-grabbing declaration spoken loudly enough to ensure that the legalistic demands of watching elders or leading authorities are met.

Double-tongued, hypocritical words, which legalistically request or extend forgiveness, do not meet the biblical requirements for true forgiveness. Compulsory words spoken insincerely or forced out under pressure do not bring about true forgiveness. Proud words that reveal anger without love do not initiate forgiveness.

Forgiveness has nothing to do with legalistic leaders or nosy Nellies; it is between God, the offended, and the offender. Forgiveness has nothing to do with human requirements; it has to do with holy ones. Forgiveness has nothing to do with form, ritual, rote, rite, or the dishonest, hollow speeches so familiar to and favored by those "ministering" in flesh; it has to do with love. Forgiveness has nothing to do with what comes out of the mind or mouth; it has to do with what proceeds from the heart (Matthew 18:35).

Repentance and open confession of sin are prerequisites to forgiveness. Forgiveness is accompanied by tenderness, compassion, and deep sorrow. Forgiveness is followed by love, peace, and hopefully, reconciliation. All of these are begun on the inside and are expressed on the outside. Therefore, it doesn't matter what the mouth says. It's what is uttered by the heart that speaks volumes.

Finally, bitterness is not a substitute for forgiveness. Bitterness comes from holding on to pain and offense, and it is often accompanied by a desire for revenge. Forgiveness is letting go of the offense and the ill will for the freedom of all involved.

While there is no good reason to continue in bitterness, there are many good reasons to forgive. A few of the most compelling ones will be covered in the next few chapters.

PART 2

THE CONSEQUENCES OF UNFORGIVENESS

Chapter 8

THE PARABLE OF

SETTLING THE ACCOUNTS

When Jesus wanted to teach inerrant, divine truth in a way that would make it immediately identifiable with and applicable to daily, human life, He told short, piercing stories called parables. In this chapter we will study one parable that stands out as a definitive description of both forgiveness and unforgiveness. In an economy of powerful words, this parable is the story of a king who wanted to settle his accounts. So that its full impact is both understood and appreciated, it is quoted here in full.

> *Therefore the kingdom of heaven is like a certain king who wanted to settle accounts with his servants. And when he had begun to settle accounts, one was brought to him who owed him ten thousand talents. But since he was not able to pay, his master commanded that he be sold, with his wife and children and all that he had, and that payment be made.*

The servant therefore fell down before him, saying, "Master, have patience with me, and I will pay you all." Then the master of that servant was moved with compassion, released him, and forgave him the debt.

But that servant went out and found one of his fellow servants who owed him a hundred denarii; and he laid hands on him and took him by the throat, saying, "Pay me what you owe!" So his fellow servant fell down at his feet and begged him, saying, "Have patience with me, and I will pay you all." And he would not, but went and threw him into prison till he should pay the debt. So when his fellow servants saw what had been done, they were very grieved, and came and told their master all that had been done. Then his master after he had called him, said to him, "You wicked servant! I forgave you all that debt because you begged me. Should you not also have had compassion on your fellow servant, just as I had pity on you?" And his master was angry, and delivered him to the torturers until he should pay all that as due to him.

So My heavenly Father also will do to you if each of you, from his heart, does not forgive his brother his trespasses. (Matthew 18:23-35 NKJV)

Surely a verse-by-verse review is in order.

Verse 23: The foundational statement is that a king, or one who is ruler of a kingdom, wanted to settle his accounts. Those who owed him and who he wished to reckon with were not strangers but his own servants. Thus, in authority over them, the king initiated proceedings.

Verse 24: Out of the vast number of servants or attendants that any king would have, one special servant was brought to him. This servant was distinguished from others by the sheer size of the amount he owed his master. His debt was 10,000 talents. In that time, a talent was considered the highest unit of currency and 10,000 was the considered to be the highest number. This indicates that the sum owed was so vast that it was almost unimaginable. Study guides and commentaries estimate the dollar value of the debt to be between ten million and three billion dollars. For instance, a telling note in the *Layman's Parallel New Testament* says that one denarius was equal to one day's wage for a laborer. There were six thousand denarii in one talent. Since the servant owed ten thousand talents, he owed sixty million denarii. Put another way, he owed sixty million days of work or over one hundred sixty thousand years of work to pay his debt.

The Pilgrim Study Bible describes this dire situation in a different way. It figures that a talent of silver was worth just under two thousand dollars and a talent of gold was worth more than thirty thousand dollars. Therefore, depending on which metal was involved, the minimum amount of indebtedness was twenty million dollars and the maximum around three hundred million dollars. Whatever the case, the point is well made that the debt was so large it could never be repaid.

While we are not told how a servant could possibly have lived such a lavish or extravagant lifestyle or made such poor business decisions as to have incurred so vast a debt, we do know he owed a fortune that no amount of effort or work would even diminish, much less erase. Nothing done and nothing offered in exchange would even make a dent in what was owed.

Verse 25: The man simply could not pay this debt. Therefore, to settle this account as best he could, the king commanded that the man, his family, and possessions be sold and the money realized from the sale be used as a small payment toward the full deficit. In so doing, he was emphasizing that even if there was no way to pay, payment was still due. Further, since he was both master and the one owed, he had the right to do whatever he chose to do to make up for his loss, even if it meant taking everything the servant had.

Verse 26: Initially, the servant acted wisely. On hearing his sentence, he did not protest or run away. He did not rebel or raise an army. He simply fell down before his master and begged for patience.

However, he then followed this act of submission by speaking rashly: *"....and I will pay you all."* A man with no money or assets, a man who was completely bankrupt, a man who had no means to raise a fortune asked for a reprieve and promised to pay his whole debt. This can only mean he did not see the situation in its true light. He was underestimating his poverty and overestimating his ability to repay the king. In essence, his promise was worthless.

Verse 27: And wonder of wonders! The unthinkable happened! That which is *"exceedingly abundantly above all that we ask or think"* (Ephesians 3:20 NKJV) happened. The king didn't just grant a delayed schedule of payment; he granted a full pardon. Through his great compassion, the king released (let go, unbound, freed, set at liberty, dismissed) the servant and forgave or canceled the whole of his debt.

What manner of king is this whose own riches and wealth allow him to write off or settle such a vast outstanding debt? What matter of man is this whose pity and compassion could loose such clemency, moving the servant from bankruptcy to blessing?

Verse 28: Now it gets even more interesting. This same servant, even in the throes of his own blessing and joy, did not learn by the example shown him. He did not do as was done to him. The same scenario is played out again but with a vast difference.

The forgiven servant went out and found a fellow servant or co-worker who owed him money. Estimated by today's value to be worth from twenty dollars to two thousand dollars, this sum was trifling compared to the amount that had just been forgiven the first servant. Yet, without compassion, the first servant grabbed the second, threatened him, and demanded full payment of the debt. The same blessed, unbound, debt-free servant had turned into an ugly oppressor.

Was this a coincidence of timing that one so recently forgiven a debt should meet a debtor? No! It was a test. And it was a test that the first servant failed miserably.

Surely this brash, unmerciful, impatient, violent man should have recognized this as a duplicate of his own earlier situation. Surely he should have seen a mirror image of his own desperation in one who was his equal. But he did not. Truly the Bible says of this servant-turned-ruler-over-his-debtor, *"For three things the earth is perturbed, yes, for four it cannot bear up: for a servant when he reigns...."* (Proverbs 30:21-22a NKJV).

Verse 29: The eerie parallel continues. As the first servant had fallen before the king, so the second servant fell before his co-worker. As the first asked for patience, so did the second. As the first promised to repay, so did the second.

Verse 30: However, this time there was no benevolent action. This time pleas for mercy fell on deaf ears. The first servant threw his colleague into jail until the debt was paid in full. This was not a case of could not forgive. The Bible specifically says, *"he **would** not"* [emphasis added]. The first servant chose not to grant his co-worker time or a reprieve; he chose not to cancel the debt. Rather than releasing him by remitting the debt, he personally threw him in prison, binding him to the debt.

Verse 31: Fortunately for the second servant (but not for the first), other servants saw what happened and reported the whole matter to the king.

Verse 32: Their belief in the goodness of their master was well founded. Immediately the king set about rectifying the situation. Making the first servant appear before him again, this second accounting was not about the original debt or money owed. This time the servant was accountable for his attitudes and actions against his fellow servant. The king considered the first servant's misconduct to be so heinous that he called him a *"wicked servant"* and reminded him that he had wholly forgiven him his debt *"because you begged me."*

Verse 33: Then the king stated the obvious. To paraphrase, "You should have learned from me and followed my example. You should have done as I did. As you were forgiven and blessed, so you should have forgiven and blessed."

Verse 34: Then the bomb dropped! Oh, what horror! Due to the servant's lack of compassion, the king reinstated the full debt. His forgiveness was canceled. His pardon was revoked. As the wicked one had done to another, so was done to him. He was turned over to the jailers until the debt he owed was paid in full. He who had extended no mercy and compassion now received none. He who had refused to forgive was not forgiven.

Verse 35: Jesus ended His parable with a moral. Forgiveness is not a creed, a theory, or a nice thought. It is a decision of will followed by an action. It is something we must do. If we do not, God will deal with us just as severely as He dealt with the unforgiving servant.

While this story is enlightening about the natural attitudes and behavior of mankind, there is another level that must be explored: the spiritual. In verses 23 through 34, the parable speaks of the offense of lack of forgiveness in connection with money and wealth. Verse 35, however, reveals what Jesus is really alluding to: the unforgiveness in people's hearts. The story is to explore our reactions in dealing with those who have sinned against us.

With this new aspect in mind, let us study the parable again, this time bringing in the divine dimension and revealing the identities of those being discussed.

Verse 23: First, we must learn who this king really is. When looked at from a New Testament point of view, the Sovereign is no longer an anonymous ruler. He has a name. In the kingdom of God that is even now within and around born again believers, Jesus is King. He is the sole Ruler of the kingdom.

Next, we must ascertain the identities of the two servants. This parable is not the story of strangers meeting for the first time. Rather, the two men who needed to settle accounts were those of the king's own household. They were those in relationship with him. They were, in fact, His servants. Just so, there comes a time when King Jesus wants to settle accounts with His servants. Since all born again believers are considered to be servants of God, then we are those servants with whom He wants to reckon.

Is this true? Are we those servants? To determine if we are really the King's servants, we each need to review our personal past to see if such a relationship exists.

As we have learned, long ago in the garden called Eden, God created a man who He named Adam. Instructed to obey God, Adam instead chose to rebel against Him. Through Adam's sin against his Creator, sin was introduced into the lives of all his descendants (Romans 5:12; 1 Corinthians 15:22). That meant that every person ever born into the human race would be born in sin. That meant that when you and I were born, we were born in sin.

In this fallen state, we were ruled by Satan. As we lived our lives, each of us followed his lead and continued to sin, adding many more sins to the original one. For each sin, account was kept. For each, payment was due. For each, "….the wages of sin is death" (Romans 6:23 NKJV).

When we finally realized our plight, that we were bound in sin and that we owed a huge debt for our sin, we came to understand that the only way we could be rid of our accumulated sin was to seek salvation through the forgiveness of our sin through the blood that Jesus shed on Calvary. In His sacrifice for us, Jesus, who was sinless, was made to be sin. He who had never committed a sin had sin placed on Him. Our sin! As our Substitute, He suffered and died in our place. Giving His life for ours, He paid the penalty for our sin by His death.

Though He had made provision for each of us, each of us was individually responsible to go to Him and to settle our outstanding account. Each of us was personally required to repent of our sins, confess them to Him, and ask Him to forgive them. As soon as we did so, Jesus forgave us and canceled all debt and obligation due because of them. Redeemed and set free from the mastery of Satan, we came under the governance of the Lord Jesus Christ. Instead of being satanic slaves, we became servants of the Most High. Like the servants in the parable, we were placed into relationship with our King. We are now members of His household.

Verse 24: As the human king decided to settle accounts, so Jesus has accounts to settle with us. But, what are these accounts?

The human king demanded accountability for debt owed him from a man who acquired the debt while in his service. Just so, since we are born again, Jesus is not asking us to again be accountable again for the transgressions committed before our salvation that have already been forgiven. Rather, our King is demanding accountability for the debt we owe Him for sins we have committed since we have been in His service.

The truth is that none of us lives without sin. Years of conditioning by the world, flesh, and the devil before salvation and lack of training, discipline, and commitment after it leave us weak in certain areas and susceptible to sin. Sometimes we fall. Not purposefully, not habitually, but as we work out our salvation, we do trespass. Just as each sin committed before salvation had to be paid for, so each sin even after our spiritual rebirth is noted, and we are responsible for it.

As Christians, we are never exempt from accountability. Just as the human king called his servant to him to reckon with him, to make adjustments, or to resolve the issue, so will our King do with each of us. If we are hindered by sin in our lives, He has the right to require us to appear before Him and to give an account of our attitudes, actions, decisions, words, and relationships. Nothing will be left out of the inquiry. And since the King knows all, nothing will be hidden from Him.

Perhaps we haven't kept good records and don't know how much we owe Him. Perhaps we have never really cared. However, the awesome, awful truth is that the commission of just one sin plunges us into debt. Divorce, drunkenness, gambling, pornography, abuse, monetary impropriety, dishonesty, laziness, and rebellion (to name but a few) are sins that have plagued the Church as well as the world. Further, failing to gain victory over areas of personal weakness or being influenced by the presence of strongholds in our lives contributes to our personal accounts. If even one sin places us in debt to God, just think how vast the account due for multiple sin is. It is a liability beyond our ability to calculate or comprehend.

Verse 25: Once confronted with both the fact of our debt and its immense size, it is humbling to admit we have no way to pay it. Acknowledging that we cannot do so forces us to focus on our poverty. Even as we are called before the One to whom our new debt is owed, we know that no amount of reasoning or bargaining will help. Any adjustments in what is due will have to be made by Him, not us. Divine debt is not payable through human means.

Since we cannot really calculate how great our debt to Jesus is, we are unable to understand how much we owe. Since we can't fathom His deep love for us, we can't figure out how to repay Him. We become aware that neither our multitudinous works nor our forfeiture of all that is dear to us will ever suffice. They are not acceptable repayment. Even offering our own lives is not enough to settle the account. There is no human premium that can be offered that will resolve the spiritual dilemma or pay the debt.

The issue here is not how the debt was accrued; it is the fact that there is debt. Since the debt is present and it is directly attributable to us, the King has the right to demand payment from us.

Verse 26: Accountability makes us very aware of position. Jesus is King; we are His servants. He is owed; we are His debtors. When we realize we cannot repay, it is good to fall before our Lord and to humble ourselves before we speak to Him.

How sad it is that even in our post-salvation accountability, so many of us still try to bargain with God. We ask for patience, as if more time would give us a human means to pay our holy debt. We promise to repay, which is simply a way of saying we will work harder to be better people. At some point, we must understand that our only recourse to settle our debt with God now is the same as it was before. The only door open to us is the door of mercy. Through Jesus Christ, a way has been made for us to be released from our present sin. *"If we confess our sins, He is faithful and just to forgive us our sins and to cleanse us from all unrighteousness"* (1 John 1:9 NKJV).

Verse 27: What amazing things happen when we touch the heart of God! When completely in over our heads or entangled in the worst of messes, an appeal to the King will bring kindness. Beseeching our Lord will yield compassion. Repenting of and confessing our sin, requesting forgiveness, and throwing ourselves on the mercy of the One we owe so much produces blessings.

First, we are loosed. That is, we are released, let go, unbound, or set at liberty from the crushing weight of our debt.

Second, we are forgiven the debt. That is, the full amount owed is canceled. Freed from all obligation regarding our debt, we do not have to pay it. The One who is owed the debt paid it.

By forgiving us, Jesus also has set a royal example. The principles of forgiving debtors are clearly shown:

1. As His servants, we must emulate our King.

2. As He did, so must we do.

3. As He forgave, so we, too, must forgive.

How high and how wide is the wealth of such a Lord that He could forgive us so much with no diminishing of His holiness or blessing? How vast is the heart of such a King that He could redeem our debt with no loss of grace or power? Can anyone measure or calculate His love and mercy for us?

Verse 28: Until now, these verses have been descriptive of the vertical relationship between King and servant or between Jesus and us. Now they begin to focus on the horizontal relationship between servant and servant or brother and brother.

The verses also emphasize human character. What was learned in the first part of the story should be applied to the second. But is it?

Has anyone more reason to celebrate than the first servant? Has anyone been so blessed? Similarly, has anyone more reason to extol the virtue of King Jesus than those of us who have been released from the incalculable, unpayable debt due for our sin? Is anyone in a better position to give testimony as to the greatness of the love and mercy of God than we who have been richly blessed by it? However, so often we, the forgiven, do not give such testimony. Our lives, decisions, and actions do not give glorious witness. The meanness and poverty of our characters tell a different story.

So often we, who have been forgiven so much, find a fellow servant of the King who has sinned against us. His debt to us is pennies compared to our debt owed to God. Even though we are Jesus' disciples, we do not follow the example of our King. Instead, we act after the manner of the first servant in the parable. We harass any one we feel has offended us. We declare he "owes us" because of his offense. Brash, unmerciful, and impatient, we can even be violent in demanding that he pay what we feel is due. In so doing, we bring troubles on ourselves.

Verse 29: When confronted with his (or her) indebtedness, one who has offended us quite often will not protest his debt. He will not pronounce our accounting unjust or declare that there is no debt owed. Sometimes, as happened with the second servant in the parable, this co-worker in the kingdom of God will humble himself before us. But then he will make the same mistake we did in our relationship with God. He will ask for patience so that he has time to pay the full debt. Thus, in both vertical and horizontal relationships, there are those who cannot understand or admit that their liability is not canceled by their good and many works.

There are those of us who have incurred unpayable debts and who think that works, self-effort, or human attribute and strength will pay all that is due. We have the same inability to admit that just like servant-against-King-offences, servant-against-servant or brother-against-brother offenses cannot be paid through human ways and means. The debt is due to sin. Unholy debt demands a holy means of repayment.

Verse 30: While the scenarios sound alike, the outcomes are polar opposites. Even though we have the example of Jesus to follow, how often do we, who like the first servant, refuse to forgive a fellow worker who is a brother or sister in Christ? How often do we, who have been released from a debt of sin so large as to literally be incalculable, fail to forgive others who have sinned against us, whether in big ways or small? How often do we, who have been released from debt, refuse to release another? How often do we, who have been granted mercy, pity, compassion, and pardon, withhold our blessings from others?

Note well! Scripture does not say the servant could not forgive. It says he would not. At times, we, too, decide not to forgive. We choose not to exercise love. In so doing, we throw our brother into prison. We tie him, bind him, and hold him in custody until we feel our requirements of the debt are paid. And in so doing, we bind ourselves to the situation for as long as it remains unsettled.

Verse 31: It cannot be more clearly stated that we do not live in a vacuum. Many things we think are private or secret are not. There are others around us who see and hear what we do. There are those who are patient with our inability but impatient with our intractability. There are also those who are grieved when our pride, stubbornness, and hard-heartedness triumph over mercy. There are also those who, when we act in unloving, unforgiving ways, will take the matter to the King in intercession.

Verse 32: For those who believe that Jesus is the God of love but not of justice, for those who believe that once we are born again there is no on-going accountability for sin, for those who believe that God can never get mad at sin or that His patience will never end, this Scripture should set the record straight. Sin is always judged and it is quickly judged.

In the parable, the king is the master of both servants. So too in life, Jesus is the Master of us, His servants; He is King over us whether we are the offended or the offender. He is always aware of all the facts concerning our lives. While the time will come when He will surely deal with the debt owed by the brother or sister who has hurt and offended us, here, as in the parable, we are the ones who receive His immediate attention. Here He is not as concerned with the offense as with our attitude and actions toward the offender. When we have not been merciful or compassionate, when we have acted violently, or when we would not forgive a friend or brother or sister in Christ, we have sinned against God and wounded His people. If we, like the first servant in the parable, have not been transformed by our own blessing of forgiveness, perhaps we, too, can be designated as a "wicked servant" who was forgiven but who will not forgive. If so, we have incurred new debt and we have new need of forgiveness.

Verse 33: The Lord reveals the real sin. In refusing to exercise mercy and compassion, we are refusing to act like Jesus. We are failing to reciprocate God's blessings to us. We are not doing to our brothers and sisters as God did to us. We gratefully received His forgiveness but then refuse to offer it. In trying to choke our brother off from God's blessings, we have become poor witnesses of His love, mercy, and grace. Essentially, the King is saying to us, "I did as you asked Me to do. However, you did not do as I asked you to do."

Verse 34: If King Jesus can detect no change in our character, no Christlikeness in our willingness to forgive, or no love shown to our fellow servants, He has every right to impose a penalty for our sin. Please understand this is not re-imposing the penalty due for original or inherited sin; rather, it is establishing the penalty due for post-salvation sin, in this case lack of forgiveness.

Perhaps Matthew Henry's new *One Volume Edition Commentary on the Whole Bible* explains it best: "This is not intended to teach us that God reverses His pardons to any but that He denies them to those that are unqualified for them." Further, Henry states: "Those that do not forgive their brother's trespasses did never truly repent of their own."

Verse 35: It is all a matter of heart. The heart is the center of the mind, will, and emotions in His people. God has determined that a forgiven heart will be visible by a transformed life. If those who are offered forgiveness won't forgive, if those who are granted mercy won't be merciful, then they bind themselves to their lack of mercy and come under the judgment of God until they have a change of heart.

Chapter 9

BONDAGE AND TORTURE

The first consequence of unforgiveness is bondage. This is reflected in the parable of the accounts: *"And his master was angry, and delivered him to the jailers until he should pay all that was due to him"* (Matthew 18:34 NKJV).

In a quick-moving series of events, the unmerciful servant found himself in trouble. When told what this vengeance-minded, violent man had done to his co-worker, *"his master was angry."* The word "angry" comes from the Greek word *orgiso*, which means provoked or to be brought to a place of anger for a good reason. It is to be exceedingly angry or to become enraged.

Since he had acted so graciously, since he had forgiven so much, and since he had set such a perfect example that had not been followed, the king was righteously provoked to anger.

Please note. This king was not expressing anger toward the second servant who owed a debt and was now in prison.

Rather, he was filled with wrath concerning the first servant who sent him there.

Can we see a parallel here? Does this parable again have a counterpart in our spiritual walk? Indeed, it does!

So many have heard and believed the lies that it is a sin to be angry (See Ephesians 4:26), that Jesus was never mad (See John 2:13-16), or that if He does get angry it could not be at us because we are saved. To refute such nonsense, there is no better Scripture than this one, Matthew 18:34, to show that there is a certain point when God does become provoked. If He has blessed us, been merciful to us, forgiven us our un-countable tally of sins, and released us from deserved punishment due them, it is His intent that we would then be both an example and an extension of His love to others. If we refuse to do so, He can and will be aroused to wrath against us. *"For the wrath of God is revealed from heaven against **all** ungodliness and unrighteousness of men, who suppress the truth in unrighteousness...."* [emphasis added] (Romans 1:18 NKJV).

Like the first servant, whenever we fail to respond to the repeated mercies that God has extended toward us or refuse to follow His example by forgiving those who have offended us, we are provoking God to wrath. As His anger rises, we, who are offending Him rather than those who have offended us, will be the target of that anger.

Next in the sequence of events in Matthew 18:34, the king acted. He canceled his pardon, revoked his forgiveness of the debt owed, and reinstated the penalty that was due. Since the first servant should have had compassion and did not, and since he would not follow his being forgiven with the forgiveness of another, he lost his blessing. That possibility also remains in the king's dealings with His saints. By unloving, unmerciful actions, we can forfeit our holy blessings.

To fully grasp the possibility of this, there are two things we must understand. First, as has been indicated, there is a difference between the initial forgiveness of the penalty due for our sin at the time of our spiritual rebirth and the subsequent forgiveness we receive as part of our on-going sanctification. Matthew 18:34 does not speak of the loss of salvation but of the loss of blessing in the course of (or refusal of) discipleship.

As the servant in the parable was in relationship to his king, so we have been brought into right relationship with our King, Jesus, when we are born again. Though initially forgiven for our sins at the time of our salvation, we are not yet perfected or mature. As His servants, we are not always Christ-like. As His servants, we sin and run up a debt. As His servants, we are not always holy and loving in dealing with fellow servants. As His servants, we sometimes fail.

While we are growing and changing, God is patient with us. He will arrange and rearrange tests for us in order to teach us His character and to cause us to yield to His example. However, if we get stuck in a certain place and refuse to budge, if we will not extend the mercies with which He has blessed us to others, then we can provoke Him to wrath and to the revocation of these blessings.

Moreover, our sins, our lack of compassion, our impatience, and our failure to forgive may rebound back on us. If we have demanded justice for real or imagined offenses, we will get justice—but not in ways we thought or desired. If we have demanded payment for the debt that those who have offended us "owe us," we may be the ones who pay the most. In truth, we can and do nullify the blessings God intended for us when we deny them to others.

In His sovereignty, God has the right to do this. However, some do not believe that God would ever reverse His pronouncements. They are fond of quoting Scriptures such as, *"…. I am the Lord, I do not change"* (Malachi 3:6 NKJV) or God is not a *"man that He should repent"* (Numbers 23:19 NKJV). Instead of understanding these verses as a description of God's eternal, unchanging character or as a definitive pronouncement that His divine laws, commands, and principles are everlasting and non-negotiable, we sometimes interpret them to be a guarantee of eternal security. Rightly asserting that God is not a capricious changeling, we wrongly declare He will never reverse Himself at any time about anything. We believe this only because we want to believe it, not because it is true.

God will never change His character. He will never change His overall plan for mankind. He will never change His doctrines or principles. It is we, His servants, who must change in our obedience to them. If He can bring us into good change by blessing us, He will do so. However, if we have violated His plan, His principles, or His person and He must bring us into good change concerning them by getting our attention in less than pleasant ways, He will do so. Even if it means temporarily revoking blessings, He will do so to bring us to our highest place in Him. In so doing, He is not changing His eternal decrees. He is changing us in our relationship to them —and to Him.

God will not change or cancel an unconditional blessing. However, if He has granted us a conditional promise or vision or mercy and we scorn or mock the gift and the Giver through bad attitudes and actions, He can and will revoke it. He doesn't do this to hurt or embarrass us; He does it to help us. God never wants to leave any of us in a place of sin. To help us see, to help us learn, to jump-start us into repentance and confession of sin, to do all that He can to make us aware that our choices are not pleasing to Him, He will not change. He will, however, shock us into changing.

When we ignore God's grace and grow hard-hearted to His blessing, we become poor witnesses of His character. The worst thing we can do is to confuse His patience with tolerance, His meekness for weakness, or His mercy for agreement with our unloving actions. He may not continue to bless when His graciousness is misunderstood by us, or by any anyone else, to be holy approval of unholy behavior.

When we provoke God, He can and will revoke His blessing to us. If we will not forgive as we have been forgiven, He can and will cancel our mercy and pardon—until we repent.

Next in sequence in the parable, the king turned the unforgiving servant over to jailers. What the servant had done to another was now done to him. His master personally delivered his servant to captivity. He personally saw to it that the man he had forgiven and freed was now jailed.

Jails are notoriously difficult sites to live in. As places of confinement, they are monuments to man's inhumanity to man. They are witnesses of crime, violence, and evil. They give testimony of guilt and shame.

If we were to read stories that describe places where people have been incarcerated through the centuries or to watch movies or television shows which depict the reality of life in prison, it doesn't take long to realize that conditions are appalling in penal institutions. If we were to seek out stories of those who have actually spent time in jail or to personally visit prisons, we could only conclude that jails are places where you would not want to be sent.

Jails are places of separation. Those in them are estranged from family and isolated from society.

Jails force change. They do not allow a normal lifestyle. Those in them have lost the privilege of freedom. They can no longer make basic decisions for themselves. They are subject to different rules, a different discipline, and a different daily regimen because they are under a different authority. In truth, life in jail is lived under the restrictions of a system of government imposed on prisoners as part of the payment for crimes committed.

Jails cells are often small, allowing little freedom of movement.

Jails can be dirty. Sometimes they are teeming with vermin and rats. Bathing and toilet facilities can be limited or non-existent. Without adequate ventilation, the stench of their own vomit or bodily refuse poisons many. Without adequate light, the darkness and dampness contaminate many. Poor food weakens inmates and polluted water sickens them.

Jails are also dangerous. Those in them are crowded and forced to live in heavily populated areas where, even when utmost caution and care are exercised, abuse abounds. In some jails there is poor or even no medical care because the prisoners are just supposed to stay there until they die.

Within the jails are jailers. Jailers are those in charge of the jail. It is their duty to keep the prison and to oversee the prisoners. They are charged with maintaining order, ensuring that basic needs are attended to, and keeping the system secure. Sometimes the jailers fulfill these duties to the best of their abilities, sometimes the jailers fail in these duties because there aren't enough resources and manpower, and sometimes the jailers deliberately neglect and abuse the prisoners.

When the servant in the parable went to jail, he was delivered to the keepers. Isolated from family and society, he had time to think about his choices. Under the authority of those he was afraid of, he had time to wish he had acted differently. Living in physical deprivation and danger, he had time to come to the conclusion that he was in jail be cause he had jailed another, that he was in bondage because he had bound another, that he was in captivity because he had incarcerated another, and that he was unforgiven because he had been unforgiving. And he had no one to blame but himself.

The parallel with the parable continues. Like the servant, we may end up in a spiritual place of restriction. We have been unmerciful, so we are sent into confinement. We have refused to forgive, so we are in a place of withdrawal. We wanted to punish others by binding them to their offenses against us, so we may find ourselves in a spiritual prison. And we have no one to blame but ourselves.

Before our salvation, we were alienated or separated from God. Sin kept us out of His presence. Estranged, we knew of Him though we were not in right relationship with Him. Our salvation changed that. Forgiveness of our sins brought us out of darkness into His light, out of the mastery of Satan into the lordship of Jesus Christ, and out of separation from God into intimate fellowship with Him.

Yet even while in relationship with Him, sin can alienate. The important difference is that it does not separate us from His abiding presence as much as from our awareness of His presence.

It was God who said to His people, *"Yes, I have loved you with an everlasting love; therefore with loving-kindness I have drawn you"* (Jeremiah 31:3 NKJV). It was God who declared, *"Be strong and of good courage, do not fear nor be afraid of them; for the LORD your God, He is the One who goes with you. He will not leave you nor forsake you"* (Deuteronomy 31:6 NKJV). It was Jesus who promised, *"....I am with you always, even to the end of the age"* (Matthew 28:20 NKJV). So He ever is.

However, the same God who loves us also has ways of hiding Himself. The same God who will never forsake us has means of removing our sense or cognition of His presence. We are out of touch with Him. We feel isolated or separated from Him. Our world telescopes to a tiny cell of life where we are no longer able to move about freely. Under discipline, we are restrained and governed by a different, higher authority.

In jail, we have a lot of time to wait on God and to discern the truth. In captivity, we sometimes discover that we are the dirty ones. We are the ones who are a stench in God's nostrils. We are the ones who have allowed sin to poison, contaminate, weaken, and sicken us. We are the ones who acted like tyrants trying to bully others into compliance to our demands for justice. And in making the choice to be unforgiving, we are the ones who have brought abuse on ourselves far beyond that which we have suffered at the hands of those who offended us. In chains and bonds, in tatters and rags, we come to realize that while God conveyed us, it was our own decisions and actions that brought us so low.

Yet, it gets worse. Other versions of Matthew 18:34 translate the word for "jailers" as "torturers."

The word "torturer" should add another dimension to our understanding of the seriousness of the situation in which the unforgiving servant found himself. Jailers are one thing. Torturers are another. While jailers administrate the policy of the prison, torturers execute or carry out the penalty of justice, often by the most vicious and cruel means that they can devise.

One who maintains a jail is not at the same level as one who delights in producing pain and terror. Torturers are authorized to make a stay in jail horrendous. Torturers are those who have been given the right to harm or to inflict pain— even extreme pain—to a prisoner's body or to cause him to suffer mental agony in soul. A visit to a medieval castle dungeon provides tangible proof of the variety and the depth of depravity under which historical prisoners were tortured. Modern day prisoners returning from foreign jails still speak about their personal distress and misery at the hands of torturers. Soldiers returning from foreign battlefields testify as to the extreme anguish and pain inflicted by the hands of enemy torturers.

The unforgiving servant of the king was in the hands of such torturers. Some jailers foster a passive existence. In this situation, if the prisoner serves his time and "keeps his nose clean," he will survive relatively unscathed until he is released from confinement. However, being in the hands of torturers indicates anything but a passive situation. The first servant was given over to tyrants. He was delivered into the hands of inquisitors. He found himself under the authority of those who had both permission and desire to harm him.

So it can be with us.

When we are in the desert of discipline at the hand of God, He may just jail us or He may allow us to be afflicted. Sadly, there are always those ready and willing to be agents of agony.

Often we can be our own torturers. When we have been given a holy example to follow and refuse to follow it or when we are made aware of personal sin but won't repent, we are actually torturing ourselves. When we disregard our consciences and ignore the warnings of the Holy Spirit about sin, we bring harm, hurt, and pain to ourselves. What about those who beat themselves up over and over again for their poor choices or the "if onlys" What about those who won't let go of anger or bitterness or depression?

In addition to self, there are others who delight in torturing us. Perhaps a family member, a neighbor, a co-worker, or a frienemy has chosen us as the target of his or her venom and wrath. Sometimes even a run in with a nasty stranger in a store or an incident of road rage can cause us pain.

Yet, there is another who delights in afflicting the saints of God. He dreams of exquisite tortures to inflict on God's children. His name is Satan.

Satan is the one whose intention from the beginning has been to keep mankind bound in sin and estranged from God. As a legalist, he also keeps accounts. Before salvation, because we had not confessed ours sins or asked Jesus to forgive them, Satan could and did count them against us.

Since we were unsaved, Satan had the right to rule us. In this state, he was our jailer, and we were under his authority. He could and did keep us in primitive, uncomfortable, dirty prisons. We also were subject to him as torturer. He could and did inflict physical disease and mental anguish on us. We were helpless to defend ourselves.

Delighted in his position of tyrant, Satan did all he could to keep us bound in sin. He fought our salvation with all his being because he knew that when we received forgiveness for our sins he would have no more legal reason to keep us in captivity and no more authority to torture us.

While it is true that Satan loses jurisdiction over us when Jesus becomes our Savior and he loses the right to govern us when we acknowledge that Jesus is our Lord, there are times when he can still afflict us. If given permission to do so by God, Satan can persecute some saints after their salvation.

From the Old Testament, consider Job, a man who was *"....blameless and upright, and one who feared God and shunned evil*" (Job 1:1 NKJV). Though Job had done nothing wrong, the Lord actually initiated a conversation with Satan (Job 1:8) which then allowed that evil one to attack, afflict, harm, and bring intense pain of body and soul to Job.

Or, consider Saul. This disobedient, rebellious king sinned against God. Proud and unyielding of heart, he refused to repent. Thus, though Saul was in the highest office of the land, God sent a distressing or tormenting spirit upon him (1 Samuel 16:14).

For those who say this is from the Old Testament and has no application to things brought under the cross in the New Covenant, ponder the story in 1 Corinthians 5. Here a man was fornicating with his father's wife (1 Corinthians 5:1). What was Paul's answer to this dilemma? As a representative of God, he told the Corinthian Church to, "*deliver such a one to Satan for the destruction of the flesh, that his spirit may be saved in the day of the Lord Jesus*" (1 Corinthians 5:5 NKJV).

If this sinful man was not a believer or a member of the Corinthian Church, neither Paul nor the Church members would have had anything to say about the situation. However, he was under Church jurisdiction and his sin was publicly known. Therefore, it was necessary to demonstrate to all who had been too tolerant of the violation of divine law just how wrong his—and their—actions were. Paul ordered the man cast out of the congregation, or excommunicated, for the purpose of destroying his flesh in order to save his spirit. He was turned over to Satan, the torturer, until the man confessed his sin, repented, and requested to be forgiven so he could be readmitted into the Church.

If forgiveness and restoration could be accomplished no other way, then it had to be done by allowing some form of demonic pain. Please understand that while the means were isolation and affliction, the purpose was not to repel but to restore. While the instrument was satanic torment, the aim was not rejection but reconciliation.

This lesson was not just for historical figures of the past. It is relevant to us today. Can we get to the place where sin, not the sin of someone else who has offended us but *our own sin* caused by our reacting badly to offense, is estranging us from our Father? Can we find ourselves in that dark area where we have refused repeated warnings and we have ignored divine example to forgive and are now arousing divine wrath? Can we ever go so far as to find ourselves in danger of being subject to demonic affliction if we are unforgiving? Paul seems to think so. In verses that deal specifically with our need to forgive, he says: *"Now whom you forgive anything, I also forgive. For if indeed I have forgiven anything, I have forgiven that one for your sakes in the presence of Christ, lest Satan should take advantage of us...."* [emphasis added] (2 Corinthians 2:10-11 NKJV).

Let it be clearly understood. Satan takes advantage of unforgiveness. In our intransigence, in our hard-heartedness, we can provoke God enough that He will turn us over to torment. Failure to forgive those who offend us is the same as binding them in their sin, putting them in captivity, and wishing satanic evil be loosed on them. If our unholy mind set, our flesh, or our demand for "justice" overrides the holy order to forgive, sometimes the only way God can get our attention is by subjecting us, at least for a season, to the very same evil and torment we have wished on them.

Wouldn't it be ironic if someday our refusal to forgive sent our offender to prison and our refusal to be forgiving sent us there too, and we found ourselves together in the same dark place? Hopefully such enforced bonding in captivity would give us the time and eventually the desire to change and to work out the problems. But wouldn't it be wonderful if we learned the blessing of forgiveness long before we sent ourselves to jail, and so we could avoid all that self-inflicted pain?

Chapter 10

REINSTATEMENT OF DEBT

U ntil now, the parable of settling the accounts has been teaching of the vertical relationship, man-to-God, in forgiveness. Now, beginning with verse twenty-eight, a whole new element is introduced: the horizontal relationship of man-to-man before God.

Bringing ourselves into bondage is not the only consequence of unforgiveness. As taught in the parable of the king who wished to settle accounts, another result is just as serious and far-reaching. While refusal to forgive arouses divine wrath, delivers us up to bondage and captivity, and subjects us to satanic torture, it also is the cause of the re-imposition of debt.

In the parable, the servant owed the king 10,000 talents, a dollar figure so vast that he, in many life times, could not have repaid it. Yet out of a heart of mercy and compassion, as an expression of pure love, the king forgave or canceled the whole debt.

However, later when the king was told that his highly favored servant had been in exactly the same position of extending forgiveness, when he learned that the servant had the same opportunity but not the desire to forgive, things changed. After the first servant refused pleas for patience from the second servant, the king also refused to be merciful to the first servant. He violently pressed the first servant for repayment for all that was due him and threw him into jail until he paid his original debt. In other words, the king revoked his pardon. The servant once again owed 10,000 talents and had to stay in jail until he paid all that was due. Since he could not pay, that "until" meant for a very long time.

So too with us. King Jesus is even more gracious with us than the king was in his first encounter with his servant. The debt we owe Jesus is due to sin in our lives. When we realize our great liability, when we understand there is nothing we can ever do to repay what is owed, when we acknowledge that Jesus has already made provision for the lifting of our burden and we ask Him to pardon us, He forgives us our debt. No matter how vast or immeasurable, no matter how excessive, enormous, or extraordinary, He, out of a heart of love and a nature of compassion, forgives us whenever we repent, confess our sins and ask him to save us from them. No part of the debt is left outstanding. No part still is owed in our account. No part is held over us or left unremitted.

However if we, as His servants, are later in a position to grant pardon to someone who has offended us or we have the opportunity to forgive a fellow servant who has run up a debt against us and we refuse to do so, things change.

If we have received holy forgiveness and then revert to the unholy by acting mercilessly toward any who offend us, we sin. If we aggressively and violently insist on payment of the debt we feel is owed us because of offense, we sin against God. In so doing, we will place ourselves in debt again, and our King will deliver us up to captivity until we pay what is owed Him.

His principle? If we will not forgive a debt owed us by others, He will reinstate the debt we owe Him. Since we have no human means, methods, ways, actions, or strengths to work off our debt, we may be in bondage or bound by our self-imposed chains for a very long time.

Perhaps knowing one principle about debt and indebtedness in the financial world will give us understanding of debt and indebtedness in the spiritual world. This principle is that a forgiven debt still exists. Even if both the debt and debtor are forgiven, the debt still exists.

For instance, if we have borrowed $25,000 from a bank, there is a very real debt we owe the bank. At our request, assets belonging to a bank were loaned to us or transferred to our account. In order to honor the financial covenant, we must, in the amount and in the way promised, pay the bank back at the agreed upon time. Until we pay the last penny of what is owed, the debt is outstanding against us.

Please understand this: even if the bank, for reasons of its own choosing, should miraculously forgive the debt or tell us we are no longer obligated to repay it, the debt still exists. Just because it is no longer our particular burden does not mean it has disappeared. Just because our slate was wiped clean does not mean the debt has ceased to be. It still exists. It is still very real. The only difference is that now the debt is on someone else's shoulders. There has simply been a transfer of ownership, but the debt is still there. In this case the bank has assumed the liability. It is on their books.

The same thing can be seen in our personal financial dealings. If we loaned a friend $100, a debt has been created. Our friend owes us this money. Though he (or she) is not accountable to us for how he uses the money, he is accountable to pay it back. Perhaps he does pay for a month or two but then payments stop. Later when approached and asked about the situation, he refuses or is unable to pay. Finally, he ignores all communication that reminds him of the debt he owes or that request repayment. Then, for whatever reason, we decide we are going to release the debt. We go to the person and, whether out of frustration with dealing with a dishonorable welcher or out of the kinder motives of love and mercy, we forgive the whole debt.

Forgiving the debt does not mean the indebtedness no longer exists. It means it no longer exists for the debtor. His (or her) obligation to settle the account no longer exists. He is no longer legally responsible to make good on the debt. He is no longer bound by any promise to pay. In being forgiven, he is free and clear of this debt and the responsibility that came with it.

However, while the debt no longer exists for the debtor, it very clearly—and often times painfully—exists to the lender of the money. It exists because the indebtedness is transferred to another person, in this case, us. It exists because we loaned money out of personal resources that will not be replenished. It exists because another, who lacked either the ability or intention to restore them, has taken and used our assets. It exists because our forgiving another means we have personally assumed the debt and are responsible to absorb the loss or to pay it off (if we have borrowed money to loan money). In reality, it means that we are out whatever amount is outstanding or unpaid of the still existent debt. The one who owed is forgiven, so now the debt is on us and we are bearing the cost.

In our walk with Christ things are different. There are debts and debtors, but money is not the issue. Sin is. And to our delight, when it is handled correctly through forgiveness, sin or debt can disappear.

As the parable in Matthew 18 connects the monetary debt of the talents owed to the king with the sin of his servant's unforgiveness, so, as Christians, we may find ourselves enmeshed in spiritual debt and in danger of sin. Specifically, in trying to settle personal accounts, we must be careful not to fall into the sin of unforgiveness. Even though someone has broken covenant with us by offending us, we do not have the right to offend God by a wrong reaction to the wounding.

WAYS TO HANDLE DEBT

Essentially, there are two ways to deal with debt: 1) demand payment and require settlement with interest; or 2) forgive it, cancel it, or declare it paid.

Debt Repayment:

With regard to demanding payment, any time an offense occurs, debt is accrued. Every time debt is accrued, payment must be made. Therefore, when someone's sin affects us, they have in a sense become indebted to us. However, sometimes during the repayment or settlement process, things do not go as smoothly as we wish they would. And often the fault is ours.

At times, in trying to get another to pay the debt he owes us, we actually move from dealing with our offender to becoming an offender. In so doing, we add sin committed by us to sin committed against us and so hinder or even halt the forgiveness process.

When someone has offended us, we often compound the problem by assuming authority we do not have. When we feel we are owed, to be sure we are paid what we feel is due or we are repaid in ways that are acceptable to us, we take on an unholy nature. First, like Satan, we become the accuser of our brother or sister. Then, as lawyers, we try the case, as jury we find our offender guilty, and as judge we pronounce sentence. Instead of allowing God to do so, we determine the penalty or that which we demand in repayment for his sin against us. We establish the penalty we feel will pay us back for our hurts and wounds. If our terms are not met and he does not pay what we have judged is right, we add to our evil by becoming the enforcer of the payment, the one who harasses the offender to make him pay the debt. If he is slow to do so, we bind him into the captivity of his debt and of our bitterness. In doing so, we bind ourselves to his sin that has hurt us—and ours that has affected him.

Bitterness is not a substitute for forgiveness. Holding or nursing a grudge is not releasing it.

If we have assumed the role of judge, then Jesus cannot be the Judge. In the courts of law here on earth, two judges do not sit on one bench. In the court of heaven, they do not either.

Jesus has clearly been given the place of Judge by God: *"For the Father judges no one, but has committed all judgment to the Son, that all should honor the Son just as they honor the Father"* (John 5:22-23 NKJV).

Why has Jesus received so great an honor? In the parable, the king was the highest figure. No one called him to account because he didn't owe anyone anything. So too with Jesus. Although He can call His servants to settle accounts, no one can call Him to do so because He owes no one. He has no debts. He has already paid the full price. Therefore, He is the only one who can judge fairly or assess the situation without partiality. If we illegally usurp His place, we are in rebellion against our Father in His decision to place judgment in Jesus' hands. Further, if we insist on being judge and so take Jesus' place, we are in rebellion against His judicial authority over us.

In the parable, the king exacted the penalty. In our situation, no matter how severe or cruel the offense against us, we are not authorized to judge, condemn, or sentence our offender. We can neither dictate the terms of his or her debt nor enforce the collection of it. That's the King's job. If we try to do so, we can be sure that we only delay payment.

Debt Forgiven:

The second way to deal with debt is to forgive it or cancel it. This is possible only if we truly understand mercy.

Jesus has commanded each of us to be merciful (Luke 6:36 NKJV). Just what is it that He is asking us to do?

A dictionary definition of mercy would include treating an offender with less severity than he deserves, forbearing to injure another when one has the power to do so, acting or having the disposition to relieve suffering, and having compassion. Several years ago a wise person gave a more succinct definition. In comparing grace and mercy, he (or she) said that grace was receiving what we do not deserve and mercy was not receiving what we do deserve.

Keeping in mind that all sin is against God, we still have to deal with the debt that was created by the nasty actions or words of others. Sometimes when we have the opportunity to make a good choice for dealing with debt by canceling or remitting it, we are hesitant to do so because we feel that such an extension of mercy is the equivalent of saying that there is no problem. We feel it will be mistaken for a denial of the offense and the very real pain we are in after we have been offended.

In truth, mercy does not contradict the fact of offense. It is not denial or tolerance of what happened nor is it permission to view our kindness as authorization to do it again. Mercy agrees that there is offense by the very fact that it reaches beyond it to declare that the offender does not have to receive what he truly deserves.

It was James who told us that, *"Mercy triumphs over judgment"* (James 2:13 NKJV). We need to follow the example of how the king dealt with his servant and how Jesus dealt with His saints. When we go to our offender in an effort to reconcile our differences, if we are able by the grace of God to temper judgment with mercy, we will be able to forgive. Yes, the offense exists. Yes, the Judge of all will not overlook the sin. But yes, if we will ask God that our offender not receive what he truly deserves, our act of mercy will open the floodgates of forgiveness. In forgiving, we can release our offender from any penalty we would impose, from us holding anything more against him, from resentment, and from blame. It would, in effect, cancel the debt.

By our action of forgiveness, the indebtedness for the situation that still exists reverts back to us. We bear or absorb the cost. We do this by prayer. We do this by seeking Jesus and asking Him, the Burden Bearer, to take it. We do this by repenting before Jesus our Savior and confessing any resentment, bitterness, or lack of forgiveness that we have felt towards the offended. We do this by asking to be forgiven. We do this by asking our Sanctifier to keep us free of any unchrist-like words, thoughts, attitudes, actions, or behavior.

To revisit Matthew 18:34, when the first servant refused to forgive the debt of the second, the king imposed a new debt on the first. This was not the trifling seventeen dollars or so that was owed servant-to-servant. Instead, it was a debt equal to his original debt. He was not reinstating debt on him for sin already forgiven; he was imposing a new but unpayable debt for new sin—the sin of unforgiveness. Can we now see the degree of importance God places on forgiveness? Can we clearly understand that God, whose heart is so vast and perfect in His love for us and who forgave us so much, expects us also to express our love through forgiveness to others? Can we truly, deeply comprehend that if we do not forgive, there is a high price to pay?

Thus, when a fellow servant of the Lord has offended us, we must be very careful. If the debt is viewed as more important than the debtor, if judgment or imposing a penalty has priority over mercy, if allowing or causing alienation takes preeminence over reconciliation, then we are in danger of offending our brother or sister. If we refuse to be merciful, if we fail to forgive a brother or sister for a very real (though in comparison to what we owe God, small) debt against us, if we refuse to forgive him as we have been forgiven, we reestablish debt with God. And when sentence is pronounced, we are in bondage and torment until the full debt is paid. If we refuse mercy, we forfeit mercy. If we deny forgiveness, we are not forgiven until we pay all that is due.

We can only understand our debtor's distress if we have been in his or her shoes. Unforgiven by God before salvation or lack of forgiveness by a saint afterwards can help us identify with his or her situation. We can only understand our debtor's forthcoming blessing of forgiveness if we have experienced it ourselves, both by Jesus and other saints. If that exhortation to forgive doesn't convince us, perhaps the words of Jesus as He sums up the parable will strike holy fear into our hearts and cause us to respond to offense with mercy and forgiveness: *"So My heavenly Father also will do to you if each of you, from his heart, does not forgive his brother his trespasses"* (Matthew 18:35 NKJV).

PART 3

PRINCIPLES OF FORGIVENESS

Chapter 11

BINDING AND LOOSING

Having discussed three major reasons why we must forgive in Chapters 8-10, we now proceed to three principles that will undergird our understanding and strengthen
our determination to forgive. The first of these is binding and
loosing.

It is good to understand that the Bible is an orderly book.
Its pages reveal our Lord in concise ways. Therefore we know
that the information about a particular topic that is addressed
in God's Word is important.

So it is with the subject of forgiveness. The parable of the
unforgiving servant is preceded by a portion of Scripture
that many of us have read, some of us understand, but few of
us practice. Yet, because it is relevant to the topic of forgiveness, we must more fully grasp its implications.

The verses in question, Matthew 16:15-19, announce the
principle of binding and loosing and indicate that binding and
loosing are a necessary part of the process of forgiveness.

They also reveal that when involved in this particular disciplinary action, extreme care must be exercised since what we do on earth has consequences in heaven.

After a short discussion about who people thought Jesus was, in Matthew 16:15-18 (NKJV) He asked His disciples who they thought He was. Specifically addressing Peter, He queried:

".... who do you say that I am?"

Simon Peter answered and said, "You are the Christ, the Son of the living God."

Jesus answered and said to him, "Blessed are you, Simon Bar-Jonah, for flesh and blood has not revealed this to you, but My Father who is in heaven. And I also say to you that you are Peter, and on this rock I will build My Church and the gates of Hades shall not prevail against it."

In direct response to Simon Peter's recognition of Jesus as *"the Christ, the Son of the living God,"* Jesus prophetically declared five startling facts:

1. *You are Peter....*The first revelation concerned the identity of Peter. As He had done with others like Abram or Jacob, the Lord changed this man's name. At the beginning of His ministry Jesus had said to Peter, *"You are Simon son of John. You shall be called Cephas—which translated is Peter [Stone]"* (John 1:42 AMP). Now Jesus was confirming His choice. As Simon had revealed Jesus' identity, so now Jesus revealed his. Simon the son of John was now Peter, a stone.

2. *....and on this rock....*The second revelation identified Jesus. He was not like Peter, one stone among many

"being built up a spiritual house, a holy priesthood, to offer up spiritual sacrifices acceptable to God through Jesus Christ" (1 Peter 2:5 NKJV). Instead, Jesus was *the* Rock, the Messiah, and the Son of God.

3. *.... I will build....* Since He was the Messiah, the Anointed One, Jesus was able to do His Father's will. Since He was the Son of God, He was willing to do his Father's will. Since He was Jesus and therefore in a special intimate relationship with His Father, He desired to do His Father's will. Since He was the Rock, the strong, massive, solid, immeasurable, immoveable One, the job of constructing something heavenly on earth would fall to Him.

4. *....My church....* That which would be built or raised up was a called out or separated out assembly of believers that would be known as the Church. In using the pronoun "My," Jesus was declaring that He was not only Builder but also Head of and Possessor of this body as well.

5. *.....and the gates of Hades shall not prevail against it.* Built on such a firm foundation, this Church would be so victorious, strong, and invincible that even the realms of Hades would not withstand, overrule, or conquer it.

Yet there was more: *"And I will give you the keys of the kingdom of heaven; and whatever you bind on earth will be bound in heaven, and whatever you loose on earth will be loosed in heaven"* (Matthew 16:19 NKJV).

The keys are for the kingdom of God. They signify the means or the authority by which to govern the kingdom in the physical absence of the King. Since Jesus gives the keys, all authority, all right to rule, and all law, ordinance, and command of rule comes from Him. Yet, in His promise to build His Church, He would include people. He would legislate and mankind would administrate the kingdom of God on earth through His body, the Church. Further, He would inextricably link those He chose and placed in administrative positions in the Church on earth with those in heaven in such a way that proper and righteous actions on earth would be affirmed and honored as such in heaven

To combine the verses, Peter, one chip or stone from the Rock, one tiny fragment chiseled or hewn from the massive Rock, who knew and acknowledged Jesus as the Christ, the Son of God, would be a leader, an apostle, in this new body called a Church. Whatever he bound or refused in the new Church would be bound in heaven. Whatever he loosed or allowed in the Church would be allowed in heaven. Whatever was Jesus talking about?

Essentially, when Jesus gave Peter the keys of the kingdom He was giving people the authority and ability to govern the new Church. While maintaining leadership over His Church, He gave the apostles the right to rule it according to the precepts they had been taught by Him when He walked the roads of Galilee with them. Knowing that the Church would need discipline, He was giving the apostles the means to receive or to exclude people from admission.

Peter and other leaders were charged to govern the kingdom by binding and loosing those in the kingdom depending on their acceptance or rejection of the represented authority of the absent King. Charles Spurgeon explains this very well.

In his book, *The King Has Come,* he says:

> The new kingdom....would have doors and keys. For practical purposes the people of God would need discipline, and the power to receive, refuse, retain, or exclude members. Of these keys our Lord says to Peter, "I will give unto thee the keys of the kingdom of heaven." Foremost among the apostles, Peter used those keys at Pentecost, when he let three thousand into the church; in Jerusalem, when he shut out Ananias and Sapphira; and at the house of Cornelius, when he admitted the Gentiles. Our Lord committed to the church the power to rule within herself for Him; not to set up doors, but to open or shut them: not to make laws, but to obey them and see them obeyed. Peter, and those for whom he spoke, became the stewards of the Lord Jesus in the church, and their acts were endorsed by their Lord. Today the Lord continues to back up the teaching and acts of His sent servants, those Peters who are pieces of the one Rock. The judgments of His church, when rightly administered, have his sanction so as to make them valid. The words of his sent servants, spoken in his name, shall be confirmed of the Lord, and shall not be, either as to promise or threatening, a mere piece of rhetoric. When he was here on earth our Lord himself personally admitted men into the select circle of disciples; but on the eve of his departure, he gave to their leading spirit and thus to them also, the power to admit others to their midst, or to dismiss them when found unworthy. Thus was the church or assembly

constituted or endowed with internal administrative authority. We cannot legislate, but we may and must administer the ordinances and statutes of the Lord; and what we do rightly in carrying out divine law in the church on earth is ratified by our Lord in heaven.

In other words, authority was given to Peter to proclaim the requirement of forgiveness of sin when Gentiles or those in the world sought admittance into the Church, and by extension he was given the authority to discipline those in sin and in need of forgiveness within the Church. To be clear that God is specifically linking binding and loosing to forgiveness, we move from Matthew 16 back to Matthew 18. Once again, it is Jesus Himself who speaks of binding and loosing and of forgiveness.

> Moreover, if your brother sins against you, go and tell him of his fault between you and him alone. If he hears you, you have gained your brother. But if he will not hear you, take with you one or two more, that by the mouth of two or three witnesses every word may be established. And if he refuses to hear them, tell it to the church. But if he refuses even to hear the church, let him be to you like a heathen and a tax collector.

> Assuredly, I say to you, whatever you bind on earth will be bound in heaven, and whatever you loose on earth will be loosed in heaven. (Matthew 18:15-18, NKJV)

While these words are similar, close inspection will reveal some differences. In Matthew 16, the words were directed to one man, Peter; in Matthew 18, they are aimed at many. In Matthew 16, they are a blessing to the universal Church; in Matthew 18, they concern activity in a local congregation. In Matthew 16, they are general is aspect; in Matthew 18, they are specific in application. They are the means given to the Church by the Lord of the Church to assure forgiveness of offenders. They are the legislation that Jesus has given and the Church must administrate concerning forgiveness.

It is important to understand from the outset that the true intent of these Scriptures is not discipline or punishment. Rather, it is that sinners be dealt with in a godly manner so they can be released from sin and restored to fellowship through forgiveness.

Please note that though the next few paragraphs use the pronouns "he" and "his," they concern both male and female saints.

According to Tyndale's *Commentary on the Gospel of Matthew*, in verse fifteen, the words "against you" do not appear in the original manuscripts. In his opinion then, this passage is more concerned with a brother in sin (*"If your brother sins...."*) than with a brother whose sin has been a personal affront to another. He believes that when any saint knows another is in sin, he must go to the offender and tell him of his wrongdoing. This saint must reprove (Luke 3:19), expose (John 3:20), or convict (John 8:46), trying to present a comparison of the right and wrong conduct expected of a believer. If he is not personally successful, there is a further process to follow.

Other Bible commentaries and study guides do include the words "against you" in this verse. With the words "against you" there, the focus is not on the one who offended, but rather on the one who has been offended (*"If your brother sins against* **you**...." [emphasis added]). In either case, these verses remain Jesus' primer on the Church's given authority to restore and reconcile its saints.

As these verses are understood today, when sin is committed in the Church, the one specifically targeted or harmed by it has steps he—and no one else—must take to resolve the issue. First, he must go to the offender to try to set things right. It is possible that the offender may not know he sinned or caused a problem. He may be truly unaware of his offense. If so, one private conversation may resolve the issue. Or through this private conversation, the one who does know he hurt another may repent and seek forgiveness. Once forgiveness is granted, the matter is settled.

However, if this private meeting does not yield the fruit of repentance on the sinner's part followed by forgiveness on the wounded one's part, then more is required. The offended must once again go to his offender, this time taking one or two others with him as witnesses. These may be eyewitnesses, those who have first-hand knowledge of the problem, or they may be those who will bear witness to the truth by giving a fair and accurate account of the situation. Hopefully, in the counsel of several saints, any misunderstandings or mistakes will be corrected. Again, the goal is repentance and confession of sin by one and forgiveness of the sinner by the other.

If this somewhat less private means fails, then the offended one is authorized to bring the matter out into the open.

He is to bring the matter to the Church for resolution. Please note, the issue is not to be brought to the pastor. It is not to be brought before a select group of elders or the board of trustees. It is not to be brought up at staff meetings within the local Church. It is not to be brought to the attention of area, district, national, or international officials outside the local Church. It is not to be discussed with others who are uninvolved over the phone, at "prayer" meetings, or in the fellowship hall. It is to be brought to the whole Church once for resolution. If the offender is still unwilling to hear, heed, admit his wrongdoing, and repent, he is chastised or bound by the Church.

To the full extent of biblical authority given to the Church, to bind someone is to seal his known trespass on him. Granting that he has been given free will and so has the option of choosing his own way, even if it is wrong, to bind is to exclude him from the fellowship of other believers who haven't decided to follow this path of sin as well. It is to censure until the erring one changes his ways. It is to remand him to the lawless way he has chosen and to let him walk in it. It is to tie or to hold or contain him in the problem without fellowship, without protection, and without counsel, hoping that such death in life will bring him to honest evaluation, repentance, and confession of sin. It is to unite him to his sin until the weight of it breaks him and he calls out to God.

Loosing is equally as powerful. When the sinner has confessed his sin to God, to loose is to unseal him and set him free. It is to endorse or to support him by receiving him back into brotherly relationship. It is to welcome him back into fellowship and Church community. It is to untie, to release, to remove all restrictions and to accept him without reservation back into the assembly of God.

The purpose of such an undertaking is not to condemn but to convict, not to reject but to reconcile. It is to provide a time out as it were until the errant one comes to a place of truthful accountability.

It is interesting that in verses fifteen through seventeen, the pronoun "you" is in the singular. In verse eighteen, it changes to the plural. This confirms that if there is offense, at first an individual is to act by going to the offender. If the offender refuses to hear, an individual is to take one or two others and go to him again. If he is still unyielding, then individual responsibility ends.

In the last part of the process "you" is plural. The pronoun "you" now means the Church. If a person is deemed guilty of offense and preliminary steps fail to restore the brother or sister, the Church is to take the next step: bind with the hope of future loosing.

While the keys Jesus gave Peter were an indication of his administrative authority in the universal body that the Lord was raising up, the keys Jesus gave to the local Church are an affirmation of its right to govern its own. They are the local Church's authority to open and to shut the doors of the Church to its members. They are the permission to allow in or to shut out, to admit or to reject. The Church can determine fellowship by opening its doors to those who obey God and keep His word, or by shutting its doors to those who willfully, habitually, openly sin.

More specifically, the keys of binding and loosing authorize—even require—the Church to refuse to allow sin to pass or to continue without rebuke. They authorize the Church to honor those who honor God by faith and obedience and to exclude, at least temporarily, those who dishonor Him by sin and lack of accountability. In essence, the keys give the Church the right to declare what is and what is not allowed in Jesus' Church and who is and who is not allowed in Jesus' Church.

Thus, if a person has been rightfully approached about sin privately, publicly, individually, and corporately but he will not agree to correction or come to repentance, he has, in essence, bound himself to that sin (2 Corinthians 6:12). The Church, in exercising its authority to bind, is allowing him to do as he chooses while at the same time doing what it has to do regarding him (2 Corinthians 6:12). It is declaring he is in sin and binding or tying him in it. Further, since what is bound on earth is bound in heaven, such action is approved or honored there, too. He is bound in sin, he is out of the fellowship of saints in his local Church, and he is out of fellowship with Jesus.

How wonderful it is that no one has to remain in this wretched state! When the disciplinary process works and the sinning one repents and seeks forgiveness, he is loosed. When Jesus forgives his sin, he is released from his bondage. He is forgiven by and readmitted into relationship with his friends. The keys open the door to fellowship in his local Church once again. And heaven, in agreement, rejoices that reconciliation and restoration have been gained.

While Jesus builds and governs His Church, it is up to His saints to administrate His Word, His will, and His way here on earth. When appropriately done in His name and with His heart, what is said on earth is honored in heaven and what is done on earth, whether binding or loosing, is validated in heaven. The problem is that such activity is not always appropriately done. Sometimes there is abuse in the process.

Probably the most widespread abuse connected with the Church's binding and loosing authority is its refusal to actually do it. Sometimes the Church ignores its responsibility to use the keys Jesus has given it to keep its fellowship of saints free from the influence of flaunted sin. Instead of undertaking any process of dealing with offenders, the Church has itself become an offender because of its refusal to love a brother enough to walk through the forgiveness process with him.

Such was the situation in Corinth. The apostle Paul was shocked that the Church community had done nothing to address the situation of a member who was engaged in known sexual sin in order to bring him to accountability. *"It is actually reported that there is sexual immorality among you, and such sexual immorality as is not even named among the Gentiles— that a man has his father's wife!"* (1 Corinthians 5:1 NKJV).

He rebuked their wrong attitude and wondered that such a one had not been bound or removed from their midst. *"And you are puffed up and have not rather mourned, that he who has done this deed might be taken away from among you"* (1 Corinthians 5:2 NKJV).

Rather than allowing the Church to continue to overlook or ignore the problem, Paul's commands were explicit: *"In*

*the name of our Lord Jesus Christ, when you are gathered to-
gether, along with my spirit, with the power of our Lord Jesus
Christ, deliver such a one to Satan for the destruction of the
flesh….*" (1 Corinthians 5:4-5a NKJV).

Why? So that the brother would be censored and punished? No! Those things would happen, but the aim or ulti-
mate goal was that he be restored: "*….that his spirit may be
saved in the day of the Lord Jesus*" (1 Corinthians 5:5b NKJV).

Paul is clear in his reason why such visible and seem-
ingly harsh action must be taken. Ignoring the problem
would bring even more trouble. "*Your glorying is not
good. Do you not know that a little leaven leavens the
whole lump?*" (1 Corinthians 5:6 NKJV)

Such action worked. Cut off from those people and things
that proved dear to him, the man repented. Rather than leaving him cut off, Paul quickly commanded the Church to reverse its decision to bind the man by loosing him. "*This punishment which was inflicted by the majority is sufficient for such
a man, so that, on the contrary, you ought rather to forgive
and comfort him, lest perhaps such a one be swallowed up with
too much sorrow. Therefore I urge you to reaffirm your love to
him*" (2 Corinthians 2:6-8 NKJV).

Another abuse connected with the Church's binding and
loosing authority is misapplying the command to bind and
loose for personal gain. Some Christians use these words as
carte blanche permission to curse those whom they disagree
with or who disagree with them. They use these words to
justify personal decisions to shun, expel, or excommunicate
those with whom they can't or won't get along. Using God's

words as a hammer, they pound others into submission. Using Jesus' keys as a threat of expulsion, they manipulate and control through fear. Such violation of the loving intent of God's ways is sacrilege.

The process of binding and loosing presupposes that there is justification for doing so. It is the fourth step of a long ordeal for good reason. The first three steps should not only provide the chance for repentance but also prove the validity of the charges against the accused.

Nowhere does the Word of God say that binding and loosing is to be the expression of personal wrath, disgust, or lack of forgiveness. Nowhere does the Word of God say that binding and loosing should be the expression of hidden motives such as anger, jealousy, maliciousness, vindictiveness, or vengeance. Nowhere does the Word of God say that binding and loosing is the means to get even with another, to humiliate another, to cause unjustifiable problems, or to get rid of a "troublemaker." Clearly, no one in the Church is authorized to act singly so no one person should attain his or her own ends or censure without merit. Just as clearly, binding and loosing is a function of the body whose collective heart after God should prevent or defy such abuse.

Let it be said that in the binding and loosing process, if there are no honest accusations, if the charges against a brother are just part of a personal vendetta or leadership's inability to guide and govern, God will not sanction them. To prevent or eliminate abuse, the four-step process must begin in honor and end in love for all involved. Since Jesus could not agree with unjustified censure, in these situations what is

bound on earth will not be honored in heaven. If there is un-
lawful procedure taking place, it will not be ratified in heaven.
Since a "sinner" cannot be bound in his sin *if there is no sin*,
binding words on earth that may cause shame and fear will
not be sanctioned in heaven.

We begin to see the solemn responsibility that Jesus has
given His Church. All precaution must be taken to ensure that
any disciplinary process that includes binding and loosing
is conducted in a way that reflects the love in the heart of
God, not the evil in the heart of man. When Jesus' keys are
used properly to open the door to censure and reproof or to
forgiveness, acceptance, and restoration, heaven will follow
suit. However, if they are inappropriately used to bring false
accusation, judgment, and condemnation, heaven will not.

Woe to those who think this evil goes unnoticed! Hear
the solemn warning of Proverbs 24:17-18 (AMP): "*Rejoice not
when your enemy falls, and let not your heart be glad when he
stumbles or is overthrown; lest the LORD see it, and it be evil
in His eyes and displease Him, and He turn away His wrath from
him [to expend it upon you, the worse offender].*"

Most difficulties between Christians can and should be
resolved by the first step of the forgiveness process. However, so often they are not. At times the offended one goes
to his offender and that person is honest enough to willingly
agree that he has sinned and then begs for patience in order
to make things right.

The offended one though, will be neither merciful nor forgiving so it is he, not the offender, who is aborting the forgiveness process.

This can be seen as we return to the parable in Matthew 18. Since these words include a description of this type of abuse, they are a shining example of the right way and wrong way to bind and loose.

In the parable, the king ordered a servant greatly indebted to him to be sold. The servant responded to this sentence by falling before his master and begging for mercy. Moved with compassion, the king not only had mercy but he also forgave the whole debt. Thus, once bound by his huge debt, the servant was now loosed from it. He was forgiven.

Sadly, this servant went out and sinned again. When faced with an identical situation in which a fellow servant owed him a sum of money, fell at his feet, asked for patience, and promised to pay, he had no mercy and did not forgive him the debt. Instead, the first servant meted out a heavy sentence similar to the one the king had once pronounced on him. He threw the second servant in prison, away from the fellowship of family and friends, and bound him to or held him to his debt until he paid it all.

Since the first servant used the key of binding in anger and vindictiveness, his action was not honored or sanctioned. Since his intent was not future forgiveness and restoration, what he bound was not bound by those in authority over him.

Rather, just the opposite was true. When the king heard what had happened, he called the first servant for another accounting. Angry that his example of forgiveness had not been followed, he imposed a heavy penalty on the unforgiving servant for his new sin.

So who was bound and who was loosed?

Similarly, when we are called before our King to give account for a specific trespass or sin, if we agree we are indebted to Him and we seek His compassion, He will richly bless us with mercy and forgiveness. Though once bound by our sin, He will forgive us or loose us from it. However, if after that we have the chance and will not grant the same grace of forgiveness to a fellow servant of the Lord, we cause ourselves harm. We bring the evil we determined for another on our own head.

When someone sins against us and we will not be compassionate and forgive him even as he is being accountable and trying to make things right, we are unbiblically, unrighteously, and illegally tying or binding him to the sin from which he wants to be free. We think we have made him our prisoner until the sentence we have imposed upon him is paid. In reality, we have sinned against him and bound ourselves.

If we persist in our sin, if we continue in our hard-heartedness, God has no choice but to act. In anger, He will reprimand us. He will imprison us for our sin of unforgiveness. We may have thought that we were binding our brother in his sin, but in reality we were imprisoning ourselves in our own.

By refusing to forgive, we have sinned against God and all that the cross stands for. We have offended our Father and our brother.

If someone sins against us and we go to him with threats of violence (Matthew 18:28) and demand payment of all that is owed and we are unmoved, unmerciful, and unforgiving when he begs for time to make things right (Matthew 18:29-30), we are now forewarned that we will once again find ourselves called into the presence of the King (Matthew 18:32). Jesus will not be pleased with our anger, pride, stubbornness, and one-sided idea of justice. Nor will He pleased with our wrong attitude and actions. Though we have been freed of the penalty of sin on us before our salvation, He can and may impose a penalty on us for any new, unrepentant sin involving unforgiveness. Bound in our sin, we will be refused deep and meaningful fellowship with Him—and with our brother—until we, not He, or until we, not he make things right. And since it is the Lord who bound us, what He has bound will be sanctioned in heaven.

When someone offends us, he is bound in that offense and not loosed until he makes himself accountable for it. If later, when he has made things right with God, we sin against that one by refusing to forgive the forgiven, we are bound in our offense and not loosed from it until we make ourselves accountable for it. It is only when we confess our own sin to God and then loose or release our brother that we can be loosed and released by our King. And since it is the Lord who has loosed us, what He has loosed will be honored in heaven.

If we won't forgive, we are not forgiven.
Unforgiveness binds us into unforgiveness.
Forgiveness looses us into the arms of our Father

Chapter 12

SOWING AND REAPING

Concerning forgiveness, God has included in His overall plan a way for His children to keep holiness within its doors and sin without. He has given His body a key which, when properly used, determines both membership and fellowship in His Church. It is clearly seen in operation in the principle of binding and loosing.

To review, the Church is supposed to be a body of holy ones, an assembly of saints who are set apart or distinctly different from those still in the world. In order to resolve the problem of brothers or sisters in Christ indulging in known habitual sin and remaining in active fellowship without a whimper of protest from the body of Christ or flaunting such evil before a watching world, God has designated His authority to His Church to act on His behalf or to do as He would do if He were yet physically present. Thus, His Church is to bind or imprison an unrepentant sinning one in his (or her) sin and exclude him from the fellowship of the saints until he has changed his mind, changed his behavior, and sought God for forgiveness. Then, when he is reestablished in right standing with the Father, God has also granted His authority to His Church to reverse the process. His Church is to release or free the repentant and changed one from his self-chosen, Church-sanctioned, heaven-honored imprisonment, to forgive him, and to restore him into the fellowship of the saints.

To ensure that the releasing of a forgiven one will be fruitful unto the maintenance of righteous relationship in the Church rather than producing contempt, mockery, accusation, and rejection of him by the Church, God has introduced a second principle. It is that of sowing and reaping.

While the principles of binding and loosing in forgiving are to bring order, discipline, and restoration to the Church, the principles of sowing and reaping in forgiveness are to warn the Church to keep a right attitude. Even while binding and loosing, the Church must guard against carnal or unholy attitudes and actions because what it sows or plants is what it will reap.

To define our terms, *Funk and Wagnalls Dictionary* informs us that to sow is to scatter, to spread abroad, or to disseminate. In a more dogmatic sense, it is to plant, to set in place, or to put in a specific position. On the other hand, to reap is to gather or to bring in. It is to receive as a result of an action, to obtain as a return or as a product of toil. It is to harvest what has been sown and grown.

Most of us are at least somewhat familiar with the agricultural process of sowing and reaping. Some farmers cast or scatter seed over large portions of ground while others inter their seeds or plants in specific locations. In either case, the reason for sowing is to bring forth foliage, herbage, crops, and vegetation. Later, when God has allowed the natural elements He created to produce plants and bring them to fruit and maturity, the farmers harvest, gather, or bring in the crop.

In essence then, as binding and loosing are opposites, so are sowing and reaping. Sowing initiates a process by scattering or dispersing. Reaping ends the process by drawing in or collecting.

Sowing and reaping play a significant role in forgiveness. If at this point we are really allowing God's Word to minister to us, we may be arriving at the conclusion that we do not know all we should know about forgiveness and that we are not doing all we are required to do about forgiving. Specifically, if we have been teachable about the parable in Matthew 18, we may now understand that our failure to release our offenders has led us into trouble and turmoil. For those of us who acknowledge that we are in bondage and are being tortured because of our unwillingness to be merciful and who admit that our choice not to forgive has brought us back under debt to our King, there is a further word of warning: Scripture limits God's on-going forgiveness to those who forgive. Or, said another way, if we sow forgiveness, we reap forgiveness; if we sow unforgiveness, we reap unforgiveness.

After salvation for inherited sin, we are expected to grow in our relationship with God and with our brothers and sisters in Christ. More mature choices are to be followed by appropriate Christ-like actions. Concerning forgiveness, God forgives us our debts as we forgive our debtors. If we refuse to forgive our debtors, He, at least temporarily, withholds forgiving us until we do so. If we will not forgive our debtors their debts, He will not forgive us our debts. If we refuse to sow forgiveness, we are, at least temporarily, not going to reap forgiveness.

Can such harsh words be true? Scripture will verify them.

One lesson on this path to understanding that sowing and reaping are tied to forgiveness can be found in Colossians 3:13 (NKJV): *"....bearing with one another, and forgiving one another, if anyone has a complaint against another; even as Christ forgave you, so you also must do."*

The book of Colossians is a short but important epistle. Written by the apostle Paul around 60 AD, it is said to be the most Christ-centered book in the Bible. The first two chapters of the book declare His supremacy in creation and redemption and the freedom He has wrought for saints. The last two chapters of the book state how we are to respond to His wonderful blessing.

Through this book we learn that in seeking Him, in availing ourselves of the salvation that is in Him, and in being reborn spiritually, there are two commands. The first: we are to put off the old man. That is, we are to understand that we are no longer in the kingdom of Satan. Neither are we in the world. As a result of God's blessing, we are in the kingdom of God. Positioned there, we are to accept that the person we once were we can no longer be and the things we once did we can no longer do. We are to break old habits that are unholy in word, thought, attitude, and deed and to refuse to indulge our carnal natures in their desire to sin.

The second command concerning our spiritual rebirth is a total contrast to the first: we are to put on the new man. We are to make adjustments, welcome the holy, learn new ways, and work according to God's divine nature that is now within us. We can do this because we are no longer walking in ignorance since we have been "....*renewed in knowledge according to the image of Him who created us....*" (Colossians 3:10 NKJV).

In putting on our new man, Paul includes some very clear directions about forgiveness. Since we are the elect of God, we cannot act like the heathen. Since we are holy, we cannot behave like the unholy. With hearts ablaze in the blessing of His love, our decisions and actions become a witness to a watching world. And, as we can see from Colossians 3:13, forgiveness is part of our testimony.

Before our salvation experience, we were both unforgiven and unforgiving. Lack of mercy and unforgiveness were a part of our old sinful way of life. However, when we put on the new man, the old is vanquished. It is to be removed. We can't act out our old nature in new times or in a new man. As new men we are changed—and changing. And since forgiveness is a major part of our new nature and our new man, we must become forgiving.

Further, these verses tell us why this change is possible and expected. We can forgive others because Christ forgave us.

Christ in His glory was born a babe. Christ in His glory grew up to be a man, *"in all points tempted as we are yet without sin"* (Hebrews 4:15 NKJV). When the time was right, Christ in His glory submitted to His Father. He allowed sin to be placed on Him and as our substitutionary sacrifice, He suffered and died in our place. Christ in His glory was buried. Finally, Christ in His glory was raised from the dead. Finally, Christ in His glory, who had made provision for the forgiveness of sin by paying the price of sin, was exalted and raised into heaven.

It is Christ who sowed forgiveness into our lives when He forgave each of us our sin when we asked Him to at the time of our spiritual rebirth. It is Christ who continues to sow forgiveness into our lives whenever we need to be forgiven and whenever we ask Him. It is Christ, the elevated and worshiped Christ, who asks us to sow forgiveness into the lives of others by forgiving them as He has forgiven us.

Since we are new men, since we are forgiven, forgiving is not an option. Even in Church, even among brothers and sisters in the Lord, there will be problems and offenses. Since we reaped forgiveness when we were born again, since we want to continue to reap forgiveness when we stumble in our walk with Christ, we must sow forgiveness.

A second lesson that shows the link between sowing and reaping and forgiveness is found in Ephesians.

Like the epistle to the saints in Colosse, Paul wrote the letter to the Church in Ephesus. While Colossians declared Christ, Ephesians is a call to Christians to understand their position in Christ and to *"walk worthy"* in it (Ephesians 4:1 NKJV). The first half of Ephesians is a prolonged and inclusive declaration of every saint's inheritance and wealth in Christ. The second half is instruction and admonition on how to appropriate and apply those blessings. It cannot be a surprise that part of the instructions to Christians who live and move and have their being in Christ (Acts 17:28) involves forgiving.

In Chapter 4 of the book of Ephesians, Paul again refers to the old and the new man. This time He is more complete and descriptive of fallen mankind. Those who are still old men:

- Walk as Gentiles walk in the futility of their minds
- Have their understanding darkened
- Are alienated from the life of God
- Are ignorant
- Are hardened of hearing
- Are past feeling
- Are given over to licentiousness
- Work uncleanness with greediness
- Have grown corrupt according to deceitful lusts
- Speak lies
- Are wrongfully angry
- Give place to the devil
- Steal
- Are idle rather than industrious
- Speak corruptly
- Grieve the Holy Spirit
- Are full of bitterness, wrath, anger, clamor, and evil speaking and nature

Brothers and sisters, we were these old men! This is only a part of what Christ died to save us from. He sacrificed Himself so we could be forgiven of these very things.

Is it any wonder, when we begin to grasp the fullness of His death, that we are exhorted to change? Is it any wonder, when we more fully understand and appreciate what He saved us from, that we are to refuse to coddle our old nature? Is it any wonder, when the blinding veil is removed from our minds, that we are forbidden to do anything to grieve, to cause pain or sorrow to, or to thwart the will of His Spirit?

Is it any wonder we are to *"....be renewed in the spirit of your mind"* (Ephesians 4:23 NKJV)? Is it any wonder we should seek to be adorned in righteousness and mantled in true holiness (Ephesians 4:24 NKJV)?

In Christ we can be as He is rather than as we were. Therefore, when we are facing those unsettling times of strife and difficulty in personal relationships or when we are offended by a brother or sister, we are empowered to handle things in a new way. As opposed to the world, which majors in ill feelings, resentment, grudges, personal feuds, and vengeance, we, as new creatures in Christ, can, *"....be kind to one another, tenderhearted, **forgiving one another,** just as God in Christ also forgave you...."* [emphasis added] (Ephesians 4:32 NKJV). That is, even in a bitter situation, we have it in us to react differently than the world does and to sow forgiveness knowing we will reap forgiveness.

Since we have a new nature, we cannot allow the old to rule. Since we are blessed with righteousness in Christ, we cannot continue to let unrighteousness be our way of life. Since we are holy, we must be different, consecrated, separating the sacred from the profane. Since Christ died to forgive us, we are enabled to and expected to forgive others.

While these Scriptures in Colossians and Ephesians are powerful in their explanation of and exhortation to forgive, they do not declare the consequence if we refuse to forgive. If the Scriptures from the epistles don't make a clear enough connection between being forgiven and then forgiving, those in the gospels surely do. In fact, those in Matthew 6 and Mark 11 are stunning in their clarity and forthrightness.

MATTHEW 6

As we learned in the words of the Lord's Prayer, we are not only asking our Father to release us from our sins or to free us from what is owed Him because of our post-salvation sin against Him, but we are also promising to bless others with the same blessing. That His will is done on earth as it is in heaven, we petition for forgiveness from heaven and promise forgiveness on earth. As we reap His blessing of forgiveness, we promise to spread it out to others.

One word in Matthew 6:12 will help us understand this more clearly. It is the word *"as."* In the Greek, the word for "as" is *hos.* According to *The Compete Word Study Dictionary of the New Testament* by Spiros Zodhiates, it is a word that qualifies or defines the action of the verb that precedes it. Therefore to *"forgive ... as"* is a request that our Father would forgive us as, or in the same way or manner that, we forgive others. It is a request that He would forgive us because or since we forgive others. It is a request that He would forgive us in comparison to or similar to the way we in turn forgive those who have offended us.

A comparison of some different translations of the Bible illustrates the point. In the King James Version and the New King James Version, the verse reads, *"And forgive us our debts as we forgive our debtors"* (Matthew 6:12). This is in the present tense and describes a tit-for-tat relationship. Forgive us as we forgive. The Amplified Version reads, *"And forgive us our debts as we also have forgiven (left, remitted and let go the debts, and given up resentment against) our debtors."* This translation is in the past tense, indicating an action already completed. Therefore, though the petition is in the present, God's answer is predicated on an action we have already completed. The Living Bible says, *"And forgive us our sins just as we have forgiven those who have sinned against us."* Here the word "just" is even more definite, meaning in the very same way or exactly like it was done.

In every case, it is seen that forgiveness involves two actions, God's and ours, to make it complete. All forgiveness is through Christ. As we seek forgiveness God will forgive us as, like, or to the degree that we forgive or have already forgiven others. In other words, it is in forgiving that we make ourselves eligible for forgiveness. Forgiving our debtors or those who have acted without love toward us positions us for forgiveness of our own sins.

It is in forgiving, God is asking us to sow the blessing of forgiveness into the life of the one who offended us. He is asking us to release him or her from any ill will, any lingering resentment, or any desire for revenge. Having done so, when we are the offender and in need of forgiveness, we can expect to reap forgiveness.

This is consistent with the principle of sowing and reaping: *"Do not be deceived, God is not mocked; for whatever a man sows, that he will also reap"* (Galatians 6:7 NKJV).

The Lord's Prayer ends with a solemn warning. With his voice exhaling holy words over the holy mountain, Jesus declared: *"For if you forgive men their trespasses, your heavenly Father will also forgive you. But if you do not forgive men their trespasses, neither will your Father forgive your trespasses"* (Matthew 6:14-15 NKJV).

Do any of us have to stay in that place where God's blessing of forgiveness is not flowing toward us? Surely not! Many of us are wise enough to know that no matter how often we have sinned against God, we can always approach our Father with a request for forgiveness. Like a child contrite but confident of being well received and loved, we can run into His open arms and cry out, "Forgive me, Abba, for not forgiving." Because of what Christ did, because we are in Christ, because we are new men, if we are sincere, our request will always be honored.

However, if our requests are insincere, God is under no obligation to respond. Our petitions for forgiveness are clearly linked with our promises to forgive -- " *forgive us our debts as we forgive*" (Matthew 6:12 NKJV). If we ask for forgiveness but refuse to forgive those who have offended us, we eliminate His forgiveness. If we break covenant with Him or fail to keep our promise, He is not required to answer our prayer. If we do not forgive, our Father will not forgive. If we withhold forgiveness from others, our Father will withhold forgiveness from us. We have blocked the flow of blessing. We will sow what we reaped.

MARK 11

If we are not yet convinced that there is a cause-and-effect relationship between forgiveness and sowing and reaping, one last Scripture may change our minds. If we don't yet believe that an action, our willful refusal to forgive others, brings about a reaction, God's refusal to forgive us, hear the words of Mark 11:25-26 (NKJV): "*And whenever you stand praying, if you have anything against anyone, forgive him, that your Father in heaven may also forgive you your trespasses. But if you do not forgive, neither will your Father in heaven forgive your trespasses."*

While these words are the same as those in Matthew 6, because they were written at a different time and in a different place, they add importance to the original word. The words that Jesus spoke in Matthew 6 were at the beginning of His public ministry in Galilee. The words that He spoke in Mark 11 were at the end of His public ministry in Jerusalem. Like bookends, they encompass His deeply important revelation about forgiveness.

As has been wisely stated, often when people are at the end of their lives or their earthly time is limited to days and hours, they assign a priority to topics and choose words carefully. That is, they place great importance on thoughts or instructions they want to leave with others and give preeminence to words by which they want others to remember them. So too with Jesus. In Jerusalem, after His triumphal entry and after cleansing the temple, would He waste time on the meaningless? Would He be flippant and frivolous? Or would He step up His teaching and show memorable signs so the lessons learned would always be remembered?

The answer is quite obvious. One day in going to the city with His disciples, Jesus used the sign of the fig tree that had withered to launch into bold teaching on forgiveness. After instructing His followers to have faith in God, to pray, and to believe in order to receive, He connected these things with forgiveness. As if declaring the requirement for such powerful prayer, each word of these verses in Mark 11:25-26 rings out:

WHENEVER — Our Father does not limit His access. Time means nothing to Him. We can come to Him day, night, sooner, later, or any time.

YOU — Jesus is making each and every person responsible to fulfill the divine command to forgive. All of us and each of us must obey Him in this.

STAND PRAYING — Jesus' word is "whenever," not "if ever." That is, He expects us to be praying. It is lovely if we are praying for ourselves asking to be forgiven of our sins and keeping our accounts up-to-date with God. It is powerful if we are praying for our enemies, forgiving them and praying blessing on them. Holding a grudge in your heart about a sin or offense will damage this time of communion with God because it is a block between your heart and His and it is a block between your heart and any who have offended.

IF YOU HAVE ANYTHING — From the smallest thing to the biggest, whether offense is perceived or very real, no matter what, no matter why

AGAINST ANYONE — No matter who

FORGIVE HIM — Release him (or her), refuse to put him in your debt, to resent him, to hold a grudge against him, or to bind yourself in anger or bitterness toward him

THAT — There is a condition declared, in order that, so that

YOUR FATHER IN HEAVEN — God Himself

MAY — Is allowed to, is released to, since we have done our part He is free to do His

ALSO — His response is in addition to ours

FORGIVE YOU (US) — Release us, refuse to put us in His debt, remit or cancel our debts

OUR TRESPASSES — Our sins

We sow forgiveness *that* we may reap forgiveness. Our choice to forgive others releases our Father to forgive us. However, the opposite is also true. Our choice not to forgive others does not release our Father to forgive us.

And so, to end with a test. Please, dear readers, read it, pray about it and answer truthfully. Where are we in the forgiving process? Are we willing to have God judge us and forgive us our sins only as we have forgiven those who have sinned against us? Have we sown forgiveness? Have we set in place the release of resentment, or let go of any ill will toward a brother or a sister who has wounded us? Have we have made ourselves eligible to reap, receive, obtain, or gather in God's forgiveness?

In the parable of the soils (Matthew 13:3-8), the sower scattered or planted his seed into several types of soil. The seed that fell by the wayside was stolen away by birds. The seed that fell in stony places could not put down roots, so when the sun beat down its roots withered away. The seed that fell in thorns got choked out; it could not grow among all the other plants. The seed that fell on good ground prospered and produced a crop for the reapers that was thirty, sixty, or one hundred times more than was planted.

Can we see the parallel? If, on our path in life, we sow forgiveness in a casual way so that it falls away, goes in one ear of the hearer and out the other, or makes no impression on the hearer, it will not be effective. If we sow forgiveness on stony ground or with a hardened heart, it will have no root, it will bear no fruit, and it will not last. If we sow forgiveness out among the cares of life, other things in life will choke it out and make it ineffective. However, if we sow forgiveness on good ground, on soil that we have worked with love, on earth that we have searched out, improved, watered, and nourished (or grown in relationship with), we will reap a bountiful crop of forgiveness.

Isn't that forgiving "as" Christ forgave?

Chapter 13

PARDON AND PENALTY

In addition to binding and loosing and sowing and reaping, there is a third general truth that relates to our understanding of and willingness to be obedient in forgiving. That is the principle of judgment, or whether we receive pardon or penalty for our sins.

Forgiveness, dealing more with our attitude than our actions, is to cease to blame another, to give up resentment, or to release from debt. However, in any court, human or holy, forgiveness is only part of the whole picture. Before forgiveness is complete, judgment, the declaration of pardon or penalty, must be considered.

To fully comprehend the issue of pardon or punishment three things must be known:

1. THERE IS NO UNKNOWN SIN

For every sin there is a consequence. It is true that in the world much crime is unaccounted for. It may be that the crime is committed but undiscovered by human authority, committed but unreported by its victims, or committed but the guilty one is never found.

Not so in the kingdom of God. To God, there is no such thing as secret sin. One of His attributes is omniscience; He knows all. He is El Roi, the God who sees everything (Genesis 16:13). The Bible tells us that He alone is wise (1 Timothy 1:17). There is nothing said or done at any time in any place by anyone that God is unaware of.

2. ALL SIN MUST BE ACCOUNTED FOR

Further, all sin, both before and after salvation, requires accountability. In human relationships, some people are honestly ignorant of their offense against others and so do not act responsibly for their sin. Others deny that their actions were sin and so refuse to be accountable. Or, in human courts of law, any number of things can happen that keep one guilty of crime from being fully and/or honestly accountable for his or her actions.

Not so in the kingdom of God. Under the Old Covenant, when an individual or a whole nation sinned, there were rites of sacrifice that had to be completed to atone for the sin. If these were ignored, the consequence was judgment and punishment (Exodus 32:34).

Under the New Covenant, He who knows all we do holds each of us personally accountable for every sin. Since He is Creator and Master, He gets to set the rules. Since we are His servants, we get to obey them. He has clearly delineated what He does and does not allow in His Word. He has pronounced what is sin and what is not. We are expected to do what God allows or commands and not to do what God forbids or proclaims as sin.

3. UNCONFESSED SIN RESULTS IN JUDGMENT

When we by faith choose to honor Him with compliance and obedience to His will for us, He blesses us. But, when we choose to live by our carnal nature and dishonor Him by rebellion and disobedience, even in His everlasting love for us, there are consequences. When any of us violates His Word or will, even in what we think is the most hidden or discreet way, God's holiness is assaulted. Thankfully, although we are accountable for every sin we commit, we are indeed blessed that God has provided a way to be forgiven for it. If we fail to avail ourselves of it, we can bring judgment on ourselves.

HUMAN COURTS OF LAW

In a human court of law, when a person commits a crime and is caught, he (or she) goes to trial. When the judicial proceedings conclude, his case is given over to a jury that determines innocence or guilt. If innocent, the judge releases him; he is set free. If guilty, the case is deliberated one last time by the judge so that a suitable punishment or sentence is determined. After the sentence is pronounced, the guilty one is either pardoned or punished.

The order:

Crime

↓

Trial

↓

Jury

↓

Judge

↙ ↘

If innocent, freed   If guilty, subject to judgment

↓

Judgment

↙ ↘

Could be pardoned through   Could be sentenced the
mercy of the court   or punished

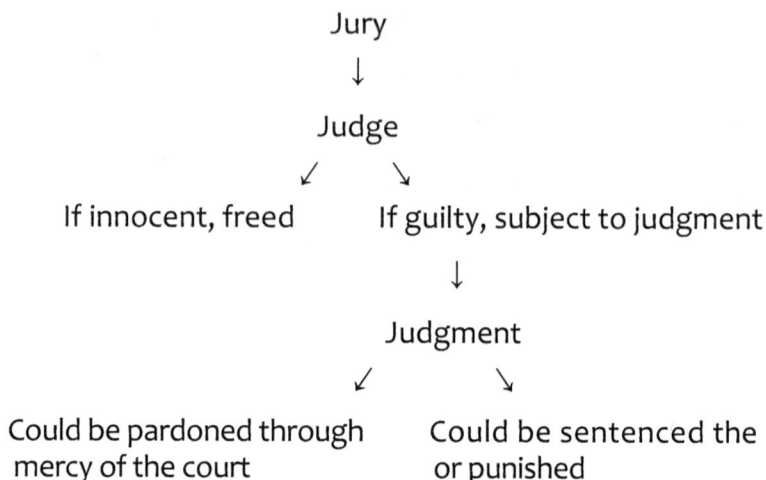

HOLY COURT OF LOVE

In God's holy court, the process is similar and yet different. When the mark has been missed, both sin and sinner are judged. In this court, however, there can be no breakdowns of justice, human failures, or contempt of the judicial system. Holy justice is taken out of the hands of man (there is no panel of peers or jury) and is solely in the province of God, the Judge. His righteousness, justice, and truth override any attempt on the part of people to bias or influence a decision of innocence, to disallow an honest verdict of guilt, and to prepare the way for divine judgment.

Do we understand that all sin requires an accounting to God? Do we realize that every sin brings us to trial before the Lord? Why? When sin has been committed, the verdict is always guilty until the offender has confessed his or her sin to God and been forgiven of it. Any exception to this would be to declare the work of the cross of Christ null and void. Therefore, any who is guilty of sin must stand before the Judge. We are not fully absolved from wrongdoing until we have been forgiven or cleansed of the sin through the blood of Jesus.

In a divine court, two things might happen. Provisionally forgiven of sin at the time of salvation, if one who has subsequently sinned is wise, he (or she) will quickly confess his sin or agree that his action has violated God's Word, name, or nature, and ask for and receive forgiveness. When he stands before the Judge he can plead the blood of Jesus and ask Jesus to declare to His Father that this confessed sin has been forgiven through that ever powerful, cleansing blood. He is judged innocent, pardoned, and set free.

The order:

Sin

↓

Judge

↓

Confess and plead the blood of Jesus

↓

Declared innocent and pardoned

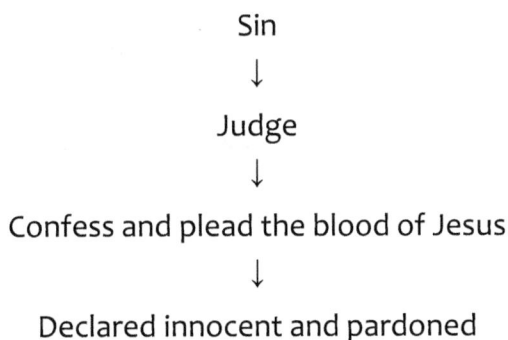

However, when sin has been committed and the sinning one refuses to confess his (or her) new sin, there is a different result. Though provisionally forgiven of sin at the time of salvation, he must still stand before the Judge. If he refuses accountability, if he will not admit the truth of his wrongdoing, if he declares his own innocence, he cannot plead the blood of Jesus for a "crime he didn't commit." Therefore, Jesus cannot tell His Father that this unconfessed sin has been accounted for. The sin stands. It is still on the books. Since the sinner has not been absolved from his sin, he stands guilty and has placed himself in the place of possible temporary judgment until he is.

The order:

Sin

↓

Judge

↓

No confession of sin

↓

Therefore no forgiveness through the blood

↓

No declaration of innocence

↓

No pardon

↓

The sin stands

↓

Possible judgment

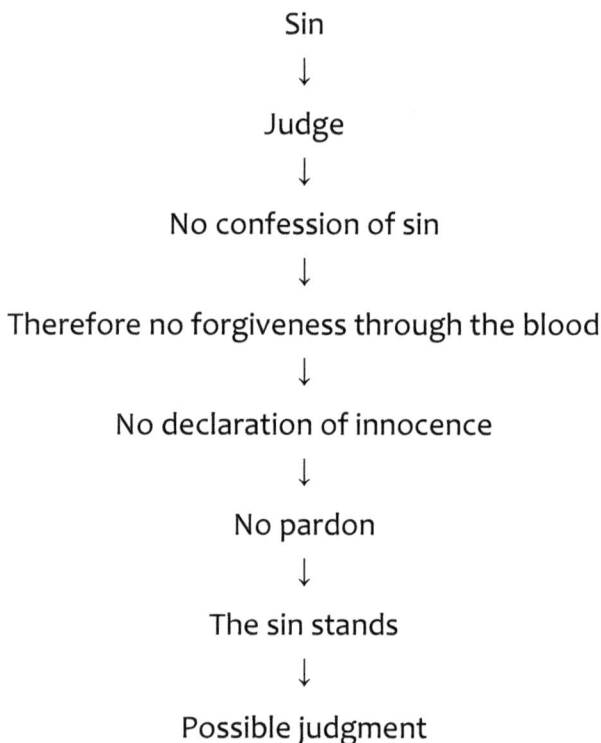

Why is it that such a large part of the Church believes that divine justice is only a one-part process: forgiveness? Why do we fail to acknowledge that, in truth, it encompasses two aspects: forgiveness and judgment? Why do we rightly believe that confessed sin results in forgiveness and pardon but wrongly assume that these two blessings are automatically available for unconfessed sin as well? Why don't we acknowledge that His choice concerning our unconfessed sin may bring judgment?

JUDGMENTS

In a human court, in the sentence phase of the trial, a judge has many choices. Among these are pardon, probation, or penalty.

According to *Funk and Wagnall's Dictionary*, to pardon is to remit the penalty of a crime, to cancel judgment, or to release from punishment. Under certain circumstances, even though a crime has been committed and a person has been tried and found guilty, the judge may pardon the offender. If there is compelling reason to do so, he or she may, by sovereign prerogative, waive the execution of sentence and allow the convicted one to go free.

Probation is a proceeding to test the character of a person convicted of a minor offense by allowing him or her to go at large under supervision. If, at any time, the convicted person transgresses the conditions of the probation, the probation is revoked and the convicted person will then suffer penalty.

Penalty is the consequence, such as paying a fine or imprisonment, which follows the transgression of law. Thus, when a law has been broken and a person has been arrested, tried, and found guilty, the trial judge has the authority to decide the penalty administered to the guilty one. By his order, the offender is not set free until the penalty assessed his or her crime is paid. In criminal court, this penalty can range from making restitution to supervised probation to jail time or even to execution, depending upon the seriousness and extent of the crime.

In God's holy court, in the sentencing phase of any trial, the Judge has many options too. Pardon, probation, and penalty are among them.

Pardon:

As Christians, we are so blessed to have a great and compassionate Judge who exercises His option to pardon as well as to penalize. For those found guilty of sin (and that's all of us), He can cancel or remit the punishment due for our sin and set us free.

For instance, at the time that each of us was reborn spiritually, we had become aware of and convicted of our innate sin or Adam's sin in us. Further, it didn't take much inward evaluation or outward observation to see that we had been driven by our sin nature to total up an additional long list of hidden or overt sins against God, each of which demanded justice and each of which required judicial proceedings and judgment.

Standing before God in our fallen state, we could not honesty offer any defense. We were guilty, and we knew it. Standing before God, in our fallen state we were cringing because we had learned that spiritual crime, called sin, demanded spiritual punishment: *"for all have sinned and fall short of the glory of God"* (Romans 3:23 NKJV), and *"the wages of sin is death"* (Romans 6:23 NKJV). Standing before God in our fallen state, we were terrified because all our attempts to find forgiveness of sin, establish right relationship with God, or earn His pleasure through good works or through using our human heritage, abilities, and talents had failed. Having confessed our sins, our only option was to throw ourselves on the mercy of the Judge and ask Him for forgiveness.

To our immense relief, we learned that all we had heard or hoped about God's love was true. He was indeed kind, compassionate, and gracious. He granted forgiveness.

Further, in our initial salvation, to our amazement, He fully pardoned us too. To our utter astonishment, our Judge was our Substitute who *".... has born our griefs (sicknesses, weaknesses, and distresses) and carried our sorrows and pains [of punishment]"* (Isaiah 53:4 AMP). As our replacement, *"....He was wounded for our transgressions, He was bruised for our guilt and iniquities; the chastisement [needful to obtain] peace and well-being for us was upon Him, and with the stripes [that wounded] Him we are healed and made whole"* (Isaiah 53:5 AMP). Since He had paid the penalty due for our sins by His death, we didn't have to.

In His deep love for us, the Judge revoked the suffering, bondage, or punishment that our pre-salvation sin deserved in order to allow us to start over. In canceling our penalty, He erased all condemnation for past sin, wiped the books clean, and declared we are not subject to His judgment in these areas again. Brought into right relationship with God, the Father, Son, and Holy Spirit, and embraced as a member of His family, we are free. Even the record of our sin is blotted out: *"As far as the east is from the west, so far has He removed our transgressions from us"* (Psalm 103:12 NKJV).

To perceive the depth of the grace granted, when our Bibles say, *"....I will be merciful to their unrighteousness, and their sins and their lawless deeds I will remember no more"*

(Hebrews 8:12 NKJV), it is not an indication that omniscient God has memory lapses. It means that even though He is fully knowledgeable of our failures and sins, He will not bring them up, hold them against us, or re-impose the penalty due for them. That is full pardon.

Yet, while God can and does pardon us for our post-salvation sins, there are times that He chooses another option. There are times when we find ourselves suffering under His judgment.

To help us understand the puzzle of pardon, we must accept a truth that a large part of the Church has refused to admit: since not all sin has to do with our initial salvation, not all sin comes under the umbrella of initial pardon. When we sin after salvation, we again become accountable for each sin and subject to God's judgment. In our sanctification process, when we repent and confess our sins, He will forgive our sins. Yet, as Judge, He will not always cancel the sentence due for our sin. For some sins, we are indeed pardoned. For some sins we are put on probation or are subject to holy discipline or restriction that is canceled if we meet His conditions. For other sins, serious enough that even though God has forgiven us or has ceased to blame us for them, we are never pardoned of the penalty assigned them. The consequences bind us as long as we live.

Probation:

Sometimes, if the situation warrants it, rather than declaring a full and immediate pardon for sins that we commit after salvation, our Judge may decree probation. Though granted mercy and forgiveness when we sought it, we are nevertheless under the disciplinary hand of God.

Probation places us under holy restriction. It forces us into a time of tests and trials whose purposes are correction and discipline. Not in jail but not fully free, we are closely watched to ensure we are abiding by any court-imposed rules and closely scrutinized to see if we have truly repented of our errant ways and questionable actions. The idea is that time, discipline, and chastening will cause us to change.

When on probation, we realize that there are things we can do and things we must not do which will affect the length and difficulty of our judgment. When we have yielded to restriction to God's satisfaction, when discipline has birthed correction, when all judicial requirements are met, and when we have matured in our area of sin and weakness, we are released into full freedom. Pardoned, we are restored to the fellowship of saints as changed in heart.

As born again saints who are forgiven and pardoned of our pre-salvation sins, in our daily walk we may have besetting sins that conquer us, habitual sins we choose to overlook, or weaknesses we refuse to deal with. Even though in some areas we are becoming conformed to the image of Christ, there are still areas where our sins cause deep wounds.

We know we can go to the Lord and be forgiven. Yet when we do, because we've been previously warned and our problem is habitual, on-going, and a mockery to our testimony of salvation from sin, we may not receive a full pardon. Instead, we may be judged and assigned a delayed pardon or a penalty or corrective punishment. In right relationship with God, we are nevertheless required to undergo a testing time to learn self-control and restraint and to gain victory over areas where we have been impatient, deficient, and vulnerable. In essence, we are temporarily subjected to a discipline which, applied over time, is meant to change our pattern of behavior from human to holy. When our Judge knows that change has happened, He releases us from judgment. When He knows we will think long and hard before we will repeat the offense that caused the discipline, we are set free.

Penalty:

In addition to total pardon and delayed pardon (probation), there is a third option available to our Judge concerning resolution of crime or sin: denial of pardon.

God has declared certain laws or principles. These are so dear, so important, and so absolute to Him that they are not to be violated under any circumstances. Since they are divine rules, they never change. Therefore, they are always to be respected and obeyed. Any violation of inviolate law is costly.

Yet even in this sphere of absolutes, divine love is in operation. There are some extenuating circumstances that determine degree of culpability and degree of punishment. For instance, those who are new lambs in the flock of God are not dealt with as severely as are maturing, established saints. Or, one who is little known or less influential in the body of Christ does not receive the same punishment as one who is well known and in public leadership (James 3:1).

Since all sin is seen and judged by God, it all requires an accounting. Depending on the circumstances, some are pardoned, some find themselves on probation, and some, when the offense is too great, are denied pardon and suffer penalty.

An example of this third, extreme consequence of sin is found in the life of David. 2 Samuel 11 tells the story of David's infamy and its tragic aftermath. Close scrutiny confirms that sometimes, although God will forgive us of our sins, He will not pardon us of our sins.

To recall, one spring when David should have gone out to battle with his army, he remained in Jerusalem. There his eyes and heart betrayed him. *"Then it happened one evening that David arose from his bed and walked on the roof of the king's house. And from the roof he saw a woman bathing, and the woman was very beautiful to behold"* (2 Samuel 11:2 NKJV).

Inquiring about this beautiful woman, he learned her name and her marital status. *"So David sent and inquired about the woman. And someone said, 'Is this not Bathsheba, the daughter of Eliam, the wife of Uriah the Hittite?'"* (2 Samuel 11:3 NKJV).

Yet, knowing that the prohibition against adultery was so absolute that it rated a place among the Ten Commandments and knowing that the ban included all times, places, and circumstances, he, the king, chose to sin anyway. *"Then David sent messengers, and took her; and she came to him, and he lay with her...."* (2 Samuel 11:4 NKJV).

Out of wedlock, a child was conceived. *"And the woman conceived; so she sent and told David, and said, 'I am with child'"* (2 Samuel 11:5 NKJV).

Still not willing to stop yielding to himself rather than to God, David upped the ante. Adultery led to more evil. Verses 6-25 reveal conspiracy, plotting, and the murder of Bathsheba's husband, Uriah.

When Uriah was conveniently out of the way, David married Bathsheba. However, *"....the thing that David had done displeased the LORD"* (2 Samuel 11:27 NKJV).

Nathan, David's prophet, went to him concerning this sin. Speaking for the Lord and naming the transgressions, he left no doubt that God was well aware of all that David had done. *"Why have you despised the commandment of the LORD, to do evil in His sight? You have killed Uriah the Hittite with the sword; you have taken his wife to be your wife, and have killed him with the sword of the people of Ammon"* (2 Samuel 12:9 NKJV).

Subsequently, David did repent. *"So David said to Nathan, 'I have sinned against the LORD'"* (2 Samuel 12:13 NKJV).

And David was forgiven. "And Nathan said to David, 'The Lord has put away your sin'" (2 Samuel 12:13 NKJV).

It is evident that God was merciful to David. Under Old Covenant law, adultery was punishable by stoning, and taking a life cost a life. In neither case did the king receive that which he deserved. Rather, God's prophet announced, *"you shall not die"* (2 Samuel 12:13 NKJV).

Yet, even though David repented and confessed his sin and even though God was merciful and forgave him and even though he was restored to relationship with God whose laws he had violated, *he was not pardoned.* Since he had long known the Lord, since he was the leader and king of the

Lord's people, David was given a harsh and far-reaching judgment.

> Now therefore, the sword shall never depart from
> your house, because you have despised Me, and
> have taken the wife of Uriah the Hittite to be your
> wife. Thus says the LORD: Behold, I will raise up ad-
> versity against you from your own house; and I will
> take your wives before your eyes and give them to
> your neighbor. And he shall lie with your wives in
> the sight of this sun. For you did it secretly, but I
> will do this thing before all Israel, before the sun.
> (2 Samuel 12:10-12 NKJV)

Since David's private sin had become public and his secret sin had become well known and since his choices and actions had been such a disgraceful and unholy witness to God's enemies, he was refused pardon. He would have to pay the penalty for his sin. "*However, because by this deed you have given great occasion to the enemies of the LORD to blaspheme, the child also who is born to you shall surely die*" (2 Samuel 12:14 NKJV).

Every bit of Nathan's word came to pass. The baby did die (2 Samuel 12:18). Further, the sword or violence never departed from David's house. One son raped his sister (2 Samuel 13:1-20) and another son, Absalom, murdered his brother Amnon (2 Samuel 13:21-36). There was adversity in David's house when Absalom plotted to take his throne (2 Samuel 15 and 16) and when David's wives were violated on a rooftop (2 Samuel 16:21-22).

Forgiven but not pardoned, David lived with the consequences of his actions to the day he died.

Whether we want to admit it or not, whether it flies in the face of our present theology or eradicates our decision to ignore the judgmental aspect of the forgiveness process, God's judgment among His people yesterday can be His judgment among His people today.

If we rebel against God's most fundamental laws, if we harm the lives of babes (both spiritual and physical) entrusted to our care, if we are slow or unwilling to repent, we may never be released from the aftermath of our sin. Even if we have received the blessing of forgiveness, it is possible to live our lives like Esau, who was unable to repent (Hebrews 12:16-17), or to endure our lives like David, who knew he would never be pardoned for his sin. We, like they, could suffer punishment for offenses until the day we die.

Penalty vs. Penance

We must understand that when we are speaking of penalty, we are not speaking of penance. A comparison is in order.

As stated, the idea of penalty is to undergo godly discipline to bring a maturing in attitude toward God and a change in our thoughts and behavior. It is part of the forgiveness-pardon process that God has provided for the forgiveness of our sins.

According to *Funk and Wagnalls Dictionary*, penance is defined as a feeling of sorrow for sin. It is said to be suffering, mortification, or piety which is imposed or voluntarily undertaken as an atonement or outward sign of the repentance for sin.

The foundational effort or aim of penance is to make amends for sin or to atone (to offer sacrifice or to suffer sufficiently to win forgiveness or to make up for an offense), to expiate (to endure the full penalty of a crime), or to propitiate (to offer a work or sacrifice that will make the governing authority kindly disposed or gracious toward the offenders for sin) through works.

As such, it contradicts Scripture which declares that *"....where there is remission (forgiveness and cancellation of the penalty) of these [sins and lawbreaking], there is no longer any offering made to atone for sin"* (Hebrews 10:18 AMP). In other words, there are no works we can do, no effort we can put forth, and no sacrifice we can make that will absolve us of sin. We can't earn forgiveness; it is a gift.

From this definition it can be seen that penalty and penance are not the same. In the religious world, penance begins with contrition or sorrow for sin. This is good. *"For godly sorrow produces repentance leading to salvation, not to be regretted; but the sorrow of the world produces death"* (2 Corinthians 7:10 NKJV). Too, in the religious world, contrition is followed by confession, the public owning or acknowledgment of sin, to a priest. This is good in the sense of taking responsibility for sin but not in the sense that such confession should be limited to one religious official. Rather, confession should be made to God and to the one(s) hurt by the sin: *"Confess your trespasses to one another, and pray for one another, that you may be healed"* (James 5:16 NKJV).

There is a clear distinction between man-originated, man-ordained religious rite of penance and the biblical reality of penalty.

1. The aim of penance is to gain forgiveness of sin or remission of the consequences of sin through works. However, as has been discussed in previous chapters, Scripture makes it clear that even if someone is under penalty, if he (or she) has confessed his sin, he has been forgiven. There is no need for works to gain what he already has.

2. In penance, the goal is to gain God's favor. However, those under penalty should be strengthened and encouraged in the knowledge that they already have God's favor or He wouldn't care enough to be disciplining them.

3. Penance is work imposed by self or by man. However, penalty is a consequence assigned by God.

4. Penance is an outward sign for the repentance of past sin. However, penalty is inward change unto the refusal of future sin.

5. Penance is an effort to change God's mind. However, penalty is God's effort to change man's heart.

6. Penance is an attempt to bypass the authority of Jehovah Tsidkenu, the Lord who Justifies (or the authority of Jesus, the one who saves us from our sins), in order to achieve forgiveness by self-effort. However, penalty is an attempt to yield to Jehovah M'keddish, the Lord our Sanctifier, to conform to the nature of Jesus Christ, and to grow more like Him.

7. Penance is self- or human-imposed suffering to earn forgiveness of sin. However, penalty is a God-imposed sanction or punishment, the aim of which is victory over sin.

Penance, then, seems to have sprung from, is connected to, and reflects the Old Testament idea of atonement for sin that was accomplished through obedience to biblically pro-scribed sacrifices, rites, and works. It is not a reflection of New Testament reality that forgiveness of sin need only be asked for and accepting it by faith.

The Old Testament idea of atonement for sin has long been superseded by the New Testament plan of forgiveness for sin. Forgiveness is not available through human effort, but it is available only through the sacrifice of Jesus Christ on the cross. Forgiveness is not an on-going self-effort but His victory to appropriate. Forgiveness is not what we can do to be free of guilt and condemnation but walking in what Jesus has already done for us. Forgiveness is not a work but a gift.

JESUS IS THE JUDGE WHO DETERMINES CONSE-QUENCES

While each of us can and must be merciful to our offenders, while each of us can and must be forgiving to those who have purposefully or unknowingly wounded us, when it comes to the execution of divine justice, none of us is the final judge; Jesus is. Where sin has been committed, the choice of par-don, probation, or penalty is a judicial decision that is His alone to make.

There are several areas of "court rooms" in life. One of these is in the social arena, another is in the human court of law, and the third is in the holy courts of heaven. Each has a ruling authority who is in charge and who makes decisions of judgment. The judges' rulings are final and cannot be changed except by a higher court.

In each of these "court rooms," we have to learn where our responsibility concerning pardon lies. Thus in a social situation, if someone should walk past us in a store and give us a hard bump, he becomes the petitioner and should respond by saying, "Pardon me." In this situation we have become the deciding authority and could answer, "Think nothing of it." Or, "It's quite all right." As the judge, our decision stands. The petitioner is pardoned.

In addition to the breaches in social law, there are the more serious issues of civil or criminal offense. When the law of the land is violated, those accused of crime must stand trial in a court of law presided over by a judge. If the defendant is found guilty, he (or she) may ask for forgiveness from his victim and all others affected by his crime, and such may be granted to him.

Yet the guilty one must still wait upon the judge concerning his decision concerning the judicial aspect of the crime. Even if the wrongdoer's crime targeted only one person, he has broken the law of the whole of society. Therefore, he is judged by one placed in authority to judge by society, and justice must be pronounced on behalf of society.

If he or she should say, "Pardon me" to the judge who is in charge of the sentencing phase of the trial, it is the right of the judge—and no one else—to respond to the verdict of guilty with an appropriate sentence of pardon or penalty.

That is, in a human court, when one accused of crime is found guilty, some such as parents, friends, or even the victim themselves, may ask for leniency. Further, the one wounded may release the defendant from personal animosity, hatred, ill will, or blame by forgiving him (or her). However, those who have acted so graciously personally are not authorized to make judgment in the court of law. Society's representatives must do that. In the penalty phase of the trial, it is not the jurisdiction of the defendant, of the victim, or his relatives, of the trial lawyers, or of the panel of jurors to declare sentence. It is the duty, responsibility, and authority of the judge alone to do so. His decision stands unless overturned by a higher court.

This procedure is true of the highest heavenly court too. When we have sinned, we can receive forgiveness through repentance and confession of our evil. However, this does not mean that we are the automatic recipients of divine pardon. After our guilty plea, we face the sentencing part of our trial. It is not our prerogative to assume or to declare our own pardon even when we have been forgiven. Nor can anyone else involved in our situation do that for us either. That is solely the right of our Judge.

Since all sin is ultimately sin against God, the judicial process for transgression takes place before a heavenly tribunal. Since Jesus is Judge, He alone can pardon, assign probation, or declare that even though forgiven, there is no pardon. Since there is no higher court or higher Judge, His ruling stands.

One problem that Christians have commonly made is to confuse the authority of human and holy courts and to assume that because of family connection, God will always intervene to rescind any unpopular (even if just) human court rulings against saints. Not so. To help us understand, a comparison reveals that human and holy courts differ in many aspects, such as place, time, goal, and jurisdiction.

A human court is limited to one geographic location and at best serves a limited number of people; no single court rules over all the world. Second, a human court is concerned with present issues, on-going trials, and contemporary measures of justice. Third, the goal of a human court is to establish truth and to promote justice on earth. Human laws and their court systems were established to deal justly with any, Christian or not, who commit crimes against human society. Fourth, men or women who qualify are judges of human courts.

To contrast, God's holy court is universal and its jurisdiction encompasses the whole world. Its concern is with eternal justice. Its goals are to establish holy truth and to be a means of dispensing divine justice. It is presided over by the Judge of all (Hebrews 12:23) or the Judge of all the earth (Genesis 18:25), who is the divine authority over all individuals and all nations. The heavenly, holy court is ruled over by the Judge of the living and the dead (Acts 10:42), the authority over every age. Its chief officer is not a human judge but the holy Judge who rules over the peoples in righteousness (Psalm 7:8). His name is Jesus.

Due to His higher authority, Jesus does in fact have the right to intervene in human courts and reverse or change the rulings of its judges. However, He does not often do so. Yes, we all have heard stories where a prisoner was miraculously set free or his sentence commuted. Yet we also know of more testimonies where this did not happen, where God did not override a human court's judgment with a pardon. Instead, He granted grace to the one penalized so he or she could fulfill conditions of judgment in the strength and presence of God.

A high profile example of this is the case of Karla Faye Tucker, who participated in a horrendous murder. Ultimately, she was arrested, tried, found guilty, and sentenced to die. While awaiting execution, Karla met the Lord, and her life was revolutionized. In Christ, she was indeed a changed person. As the time approached for her sentence to be carried out, many asked for her execution to be canceled. It was not. Many called on God to intervene and to overturn the ruling of the human court. He did not. Though forgiven by Jesus in holy court, she was still subject to the sentence of the criminal court. Since no higher judgment changed the lower court's ruling, since God chose to honor human justice, Karla was put to death. Yet, no longer on earth, she is in the arms of the Lord.

In an even more infamous case, Jesus was tried before a Roman court of law. In a complete miscarriage of justice, even though He was innocent of any crime, He was sentenced to die. God did not intervene with a different verdict. He did not override the announced sentence by granting Jesus a pardon. Rather, using injustice to establish and to fulfill justice, He allowed Jesus to die. Jesus' legacy is our justification.

We are not the first to fail to understand the importance of judgment that brings pardon or punishment as a valid part of the forgiveness process. We are not the first to fail to re-alize that personal or societal declarations of pardon are al-ways subject to review by a higher Judge. We are not the first to fail to acknowledge that even after we receive or extend forgiveness, the wheels of divine justice continue to turn, and we are subject to them.

Even in the parable of Matthew 18, the issue of pardon was at first unknown or ignored. When the king demanded payment of the 10,000 talents owed him, his servant was not able to pay; he was found guilty. In response, the king's judgment was to assign punishment (Matthew 18:25). At this, the servant fell down before the king and begged for mercy: *"Master, have patience with me...."* (Matthew 18:26 NKJV). Then, he promised to work off the debt: *"....I will pay you all"* (Matthew 18:26 NKJV). In all of this, he never asked for par-don.

However, moved by his plight, the king extended grace and pardoned him: *"Then the master of that servant was moved with compassion, [and] released him"* (Matthew 18:27 NKJV). He also granted forgiveness: *"....and forgave him the debt"* (Matthew 18:27 NKJV). As judge or ruling authority of the situation, the king made a decision, and his word was law. Even at a great personal loss, he forgave and pardoned his servant.

Yet when this blessed servant became involved in a simi-lar situation with a fellow worker who owed him money, he did not act in like manner. When he would not forgive a much smaller debt and when he sentenced rather than pardoned his brother, the king intervened as a higher authority. He reopened the case, re-judged the first servant, and revoked his pardon by reinstating the debt (Matthew 18:34). Through his own smallness of character and his refusal to grant forgiveness and pardon, the once-free servant was under judgment. He lost his pardon by refusing to pardon.

Some lessons are learned from this story. For instance, when we Christians, already pardoned for our pre-salvation sin, are called before our King to make an account of the debt we owe Him for post-salvation sins, we know to request the forgiveness that He is gracious to grant. But how many of us, like the servant, fail to ask for pardon? Under the right conditions, our Judge who "....is able to do exceedingly abundantly above all that we ask or think...." (Ephesians 3:20 NKJV), would delight to pardon us.

Or, how many of us fail to understand that the responsibility to pardon or to assign sentence for wrongdoing is not ours? Yes, we can and must pardon those who repent of social infractions against us. In criminal court, we can choose to grant forgiveness to those whose activities have affected us, knowing that when we do so, our responsibility ends. However, the criminal is still subject to the demands for justice by the court system.

Just so, as members of the family of God, justice is not our responsibility. As Christians, we have been commanded to extend forgiveness, but when sin is involved, we have never been given the divine authority to judge or to pardon. Since all sin is against God, all sin must meet His, not our, demands for justice. When the inevitable offense from a brother or sister comes and we grant forgiveness, our responsibility ends.

While we are set free of any entanglement with sin or sinner, our offender, like the servant in the parable, still faces the judgment of holy God.

Another lesson from the parable in Matthew 18 involves our decisions. How many of us fail to see that we can make things a lot easier on ourselves by our own choices? Our immature commission of occasional sin may end in an issue of holy pardon. Our on-going, habitual sin committed when we've been Christians long enough to know better may result in probation or a time of chastening and correction. However, our purposeful violation of divine laws, such as those concerning forgiveness, may result in a judgment of long-term suffering. For such, there may be no pardon.

God is zealously conscious of our relationships with our brothers and sisters in Christ. When we violate them through lack of forgiveness, we stand subject to divine, judicial review. If we do not act toward others as our King did toward us, we bring judgment on ourselves. If, like the unforgiving servant, we are unrelenting and try to subject our brothers and sisters to our own terms of judgment, that could cause the Lord and Judge of all to cancel our pardon (but not our forgiveness) for our sin and to assign us a penalty or suffering due it as long as we live.

Shown forgiveness and pardon by Jesus, the Church should forgive as well. If we have not shown forgiveness in our relationships with others, we may be undergoing probation or be in a time of trial whose purpose is correction. We may be under watch, scrutiny, and supervision until we repent of our errant ways and questionable actions. We may be in a time of discipline and chastening whose intent is to cause us to change—or to become more like our Groom.

PART 4

THE PATH TOWARD FORGIVENESS

INTRODUCTION TWO

M any of us may be realizing that we have long confused the issues of forgiveness and pardon, believed they were the same, or thought humans were in authority over both. Now, it may be dawning on us that our ignorance about them has hindered our relationship with God and with our fellow man.

In fact, would an honest self-evaluation reveal that there has been a decided reluctance to forgive in those of us who have not known that forgiveness is a two-part process involving forgiveness on man's part and judgment on God's part? Would it also show that there has been a refusal to forgive in those of us who have not understood the inevitability of holy, not human justice?

To find out if we fall into the category of the unforgiving, here is our own primitive and private test. Have we forgiven if we:

1. ... are still resenting another and blaming him (or her) for offending us?

2. ... can't dismiss the situation from our minds?

3. ... are obsessing about the injury done and who did it?

4. ... in passive avoidance or open hostility, have broken off relationship with our offender?

5. ...are angry that the one who hurt us doesn't seem to be suffering any apparent consequences of his (or her) evil actions while we are left to pick up the pieces of our smashed lives?

Are we leaving judgment in God's capable hands if we:

1. ...feel another is indebted to us, and we won't be satisfied until he or she has made the account good?

2. ...are just waiting until "he gets what he deserves"?

3. ...feel that forgiving is letting our offender off the hook, could be seen as a sign of approval for his (or her) wrong behavior or, at the very least, be mistaken as an indication that we are willing to allow him (or her) to continue to offend us in this way?

4. ... find ourselves constantly rehearsing the full details of the situation with God so He knows all the reasons He should hammer our offender?

5. ...hear ourselves saying vindictive things like, "You get her, God!" or "It's not over until it's over!"?

If the answer to any of these questions is yes, we have work to do concerning our attitudes and actions. Why do we feel this way? Why are we hindering, if not halting, the forward movement of our lives by our inward thoughts of revenge? Why are we so eager to inflict wound for wound? Why are we seeking permission to hurt another as we have been hurt by another—or pushing God to do it for us?

It may be worth some moments of our time to learn from where such unholy attitudes and unbiblical words have arisen. In many cases, our present deficiencies go back to our roots. That is, we may find their source in family or even religious upbringing. For instance, if we were raised in homes whose hallmark for dealing with offence was to nurse resentment and bitterness or, at the opposite end of the spectrum, to engage in vengeance and retaliation, we may find very difficult it in our natural strength to reject this patterning and to practice forgiveness.

On the other hand, if we grew up in churches that taught and modeled the atonement of sins that existed under Old Testament law, we may never have realized our need to change by submitting to New Testament grace and forgiveness of sins. While claiming to be New Covenant people, our lives prove we are walking in the ways of the Old.

Since many things have contributed to the dilemma, our path to forgiveness may therefore be a long one. When we are offended, we must learn to deal with our emotions, choose which covenant we are under, renew our minds, and follow biblically-outlined procedures. Let us be encouraged on this path to forgiveness and forgiving knowing, when we stumble as we walk along, that God is always with us, lifting us, and urging us on. Forgiveness is a path we will walk on throughout our lifetimes.

Let's begin!

Chapter 14

REIGNING IN EMOTIONS

If we have not grown up in homes that encourage valid and balanced expression of mind, will, and emotions, or have never gained personal victory over both the negative feelings and the inappropriate communication of these feelings, the chances are high that we do not forgive as we have been forgiven. In fact, often we cannot.

Concerning our emotions, we are each created a three part being: spirit, soul, and body (1 Thessalonians 5:23). The second part, our soul, also is made up of three major divisions: intellect, emotion, and will. These make up our personality and nature and those aspects of us that think, feel, and decide what we do or how we act.

Our behavior is often the end product of the functioning of our souls. In other words, our actions or reactions to things don't just happen. Like forgiveness, they are the fruit of a multi-step process. Depending on the circumstances, this process can be long or nearly instantaneous. When something unpleasant happens to us, we think about it. Our thoughts generate feelings. Our feelings influence or even determine our choice of what to say or do about the provocation. Our will initiates our behavioral response. Thus, when an incident occurs which we think (intellect) is wrong or offensive, we may get angry (emotion) and decide (will) to react in an un-holy way. Our inappropriate behavior bears witness that we are dealing with offense on an emotional plane.

In the realms of forgiveness (or lack of it), the two most obvious emotions that hinder our desire to stop blaming oth-ers for their offenses and that quash our ability to release others from on-going resentment are anger and fear.

Generally speaking, anger can be defined as violent pas-sion or sudden strong displeasure. It is to become inflamed. In its full range of expression, it can go from displeasure, irritation, frustration, and impatience to much more vola-tile manifestations such as animosity, ire, rage, fury, wrath, and violence. It's easy to see that anyone who continues to brood over an offense and to rehearse its hurt (resentment) or whose rage has driven him (or her) beyond the boundaries of caution or healthy response cannot truly forgive.

Fear is an emotion provoked by threatened evil or im-pending pain accompanied by a desire to avoid both. Here again, expressions of fear are many. They include doubt, un-easiness, apprehension, dread, and anxiety on the mental side and fright, horror, panic, and terror on the physical. It is obvious that anyone who is afraid of his or her offenders or of what they might do, who avoids or hides from them rather than seek them out, or who would find any reason not to con-front them has not really forgiven.

Without question, when God oversaw the creation of men and women, He blessed His creatures with feelings. While it was His decision to make us a people with emotion, He left the choice of the proper expression of emotion up to us. It is His desire that we choose to show our feelings in God-like ways. Sometimes this happens, and sometimes it does not.

Our model for righteous expression of emotion is found in the Man, Jesus Christ. Without question, He was filled with righteous anger and expressed it is a way that was acceptable to His Father when He "*....went into the temple of God and drove out all those who bought and sold in the temple, and overturned the tables of the moneychangers and the seats of those who sold doves*" (Matthew 21:12 NKJV). Further, Jesus expressed His sorrow in the right way. At Lazarus' tomb, one of the most succinct and revealing Scripture verses tells us, "*Jesus wept*" (John 11:35 NKJV). In Gethsemane, His soul was, "*....exceedingly sorrowful, even to death*" (Matthew 26:38 NKJV).

While Jesus did fear or reverence His Father, He never displayed a fear of people. In fact, so desirous was He that people should not fear other people, He often cautioned His listeners against such unholy fear (Matthew 10:31; Luke 5:10; 12:32, etc.).

Even if our Father gave us emotions and Jesus showed us how to express them righteously, sometimes, when we are engulfed in them, our behavior reflects neither our Creator nor His Representative. When anger and fear in our souls are not dealt with, it is difficult to forgive. When they have long been entrenched within, to some degree they begin to rule our inner beings. When they dominate our thoughts and will rather than remain a balanced part of our souls, they nullify our ability to forgive. When they alone determine our behavior or response to provocation and offense, the result is usually anything but holy.

Reacting from the unbalanced emotion keeps us in the subjective rather than bringing us into the objective. Due to their urgency, it is very difficult to be impartial when we need to be forgiving. Reacting from emotions that have not been restricted to holy, Christ-like expression keeps our feelings raw and painful. If we are not free from ungodly, carnal feelings, it is hard to release others from them either. Under such circumstances, we cannot forgive.

Further, as has been well said, forgiveness is not a feeling. In reality, it is not a function of our mind or emotion but of our wills. We don't think to forgive. We don't feel to forgive. We decide to forgive. No matter what we think of our offender, no matter now we feel about him or her, we must choose to forgive. It is in overcoming the protests of our mind and the screams of outrage in our feelings, in continuing to decide to free our offender of our hostile thoughts and emotions, in choosing to give up resentment, in electing to release him or her from any debt he or she might owe us, that we truly forgive.

The God who gave us emotions expects us to use them if we are to experience life at its fullest. It is not the emotions themselves but their imbalance, not the feelings themselves but our immature or unholy ways of expressing them, that cause problems in forgiving. However, when we line up our minds with the mind of Christ (1 Corinthians 2:16) and our emotions with the affections of Christ, we will find it easier to make a decision of our will based on the will of God. When our emotions have been reigned in to both appropriate balance and expression, then we can and will forgive.

So how do we forgive? We give up our "right" to be angry. We reject the emotions of anger and fear and act from our will. We confess to God any unholy expressions of emotion that have caused us to act against our offenders in an unrighteousness way (and by so doing, sin against God), and we seek His forgiveness. We release our offenders into the freedom of our forgiveness. We praise the Lord.

Chapter 15

CHOOSING BETWEEN THE

OLD OR NEW COVENANT

Out of balance emotions are not the only cause of our difficulties in forgiving. Another problem that hinders us is our refusal to change from Old Covenant law to New Covenant grace, especially in matters of justice.

Our Bibles begin with the account of God creating all things. Climaxing the amazing series of events was His creation of mankind. When disaster struck in Eden and Adam and Eve fell, a downward spiral of sin and evil quickly followed. Most of us are all too familiar with the ensuing accounts of Cain and Abel, Noah and the flood, and the tower of Babel. However, the way for change from this black morass is glimpsed in chapter twelve of the book of Genesis. There we are introduced to a man named Abram.

God met with Abram and promised to make him a great nation (Genesis 12:2). Underscoring the sureness and solemnity of His words, He cut covenant with him, sealing it with blood (Genesis 17). To keep His word that childless Abram would have descendants to inherit the promised land (Genesis 13:15), long after the time when he or his wife Sarah could have naturally produced a child, God miraculously caused them to birth a son, Isaac (Genesis 21). Isaac became the father of Jacob, and Jacob the father of Joseph, who was sold into slavery in Egypt.

When famine threatened to devour them, some brothers of Joseph went to Egypt for food and there discovered that Joseph had become the second most important and influential official in the land. Soon, the whole of Jacob's family moved to Egypt, where at first they were wonderfully welcomed and well treated. However, as the years went on, they fell out of favor.

Forced into slavery, the Hebrews were subject to harsh and brutal treatment. When God answered their cries, He miraculously led them out of the land of their torment to Mount Sinai. There, God cut another covenant with those He had called and chosen as His people. He spoke forth what have become known as the Ten Commandments (Exodus 20). Then He issued a series of laws, statutes, and ordinances. These authoritative rules were to govern the Hebrews' relationships both with God and with each other.

Fracturing or breaking any part of the law was considered the same as breaking the whole of it. Any time the law was violated, certain things had to be done. To atone for sin and to repair the breech in his or her relationship with God, an offender had to go to the temple and offer sacrifice for sin. This required act of humbleness was supposed to foster caution in the Hebrews' future choices of behavior.

When sin had caused problems in relationships with other people, there was an additional requirement. All offenders were subject to the stated judgments in the laws God had given. These could range from making restitution for minor offenses to the giving up of life for the greatest of offenses.

These laws were meant to prohibit sin, limit punishment, and promote justice. Yet somehow over the years, a different, unholy idea emerged. Justice became associated with the idea of vengeance and retribution. Even by today's understanding and interpretation, some of the most well-known judicial Scriptures seem to be carte blanche permission for a victim to get even with his enemy. For example, *"….you shall give life for life, eye for eye, tooth for tooth, hand for hand, foot for foot, burn for burn, wound for wound, stripe for stripe"* (Exodus 21:23-25 NKJV).

In truth, requirements for justice were not intended to be an encouragement for the aggrieved party to act out anger and hatred. Instead, they were a reminder of the limitations and restrictions God placed on those under the law. If we read these words (or others like them) in this limiting light, several things become apparent to us.

1. Under the Old Covenant, all Hebrews lived under the Law. Everyone, from peasant to king, was required to keep all laws. On the positive side, living under and obeying the law brought the protection of the law. On a more negative note, if an offense occurred and someone of-

fended against his or her fellow Hebrew, there were inevitable consequences. Those who lived by the law could ask that justice be met according to the law. The offended one could demand the full penalty for that offense as written in the law to be charged against his or her offender.

2. Under the Old Covenant, when there was a need for justice to be met, both offender and offended were subject to the exhaustive and inclusive law. There was absolutely no allowance for personal vengeance. Justice was not met according to human emotion or demand. Even thousands of years ago, there was no "taking the law into your own hands" and no misapplication of the law for personal reasons. Leviticus 19:17-18 (NKJV) makes this clear: "*You shall not hate your brother in your heart. You shall surely rebuke your neighbor, and not bear sin because of him. You shall not take vengeance, nor bear any grudge against the children of your people, but you shall love your neighbor as yourself: I am the LORD.*"

3. Under the Old Covenant, in matters of personal justice, only the person responsible for law breaking was punished. There was to be no inclusion of the innocent in punishment meted out to the guilty. For example, "*....and if a man beats his male or female servant with a rod, so that he dies under his hand, **he** shall surely be*

*punished ... If men fight, and hurt a woman with child, so that she gives birth prematurely, yet no lasting harm follows, **he** shall surely be punished...."* [emphasis added] (Exodus 21: 20, 22 NKJV).

4. Under the Old Covenant, punishment was limited by and to the law. It was to be equal to or not to exceed the damage done as determined by law. Thus, in their true intent, the words, *"an eye for an eye"* (Matthew 5:38 NKJV) were not an exhortation to full scale mayhem. Rather, by allowing room for honest pursuit of justice, they clearly prohibit even a minute escalation of personal vindictiveness and revenge and forbid individual excess or violence.

5. Under the Old Covenant, all justice with its subsequent pardon or punishment originated with and was the domain of God. Through Moses, when God said, *"Vengeance is Mine, and recompense"* (Deuteronomy 32:35 NKJV), He meant it. To decide issues of law and to reveal His rulings concerning justice on earth, God raised up human judges whose job was to *"make known the statutes of God and His laws"* (Exodus 18:16 NKJV).

When an offense occurred, each individual or the head of the family had to present his case to the judge who sat in judgment and who assigned consequences. In no case could judgment be made by the one wronged. The victim was never to decide a fit punishment or impose demands on his or her offender.

The ideas that the law limited revenge and that it restricted payback for violence committed against man by man were radical for the Old Covenant culture into which they were introduced. They went completely against the belief and behavior of the day where it was the norm to pay back a wound with a more serious wound or a murder with murder and to include innocent family members in the escalating savagery.

The Old Covenant with this system of law lasted 1500 years from the issuance of the Law at Mount Sinai to the coming of Christ. Fortunately, it was never meant to be permanent. When its goals of making people aware of sin, of their inability to conquer sin, and of their need of a Savior were met, it was changed.

Though the law was perfect, its practice was marked by actions of flesh and human weakness. Even today, we can see some of its areas of fleshly failure, such as when the wrong person is accused of or punished for a crime, when the punishment far exceeds the crime, and when the truly guilty go free through technicalities of the law.

Hundreds of years later after the giving of the Law, the desire that men and women should leave vengeance in God's hands, refuse to engage in any action that would hurt their offender, and meet offense with forgiveness were sweeping for the New Covenant culture into which they were introduced.

When Christ came, He cut a New Covenant and sealed it with His own blood (Matthew 26:28). While the Church is still bound by the holy principles set forth in the Law, it is not now and never has been under the bondage of works and flesh by which the Law was kept. Though it was the way of life for His chosen people long ago, it has now been declared obsolete:

> But now He has obtained a more excellent ministry, inasmuch as He is also Mediator of a better covenant, which was established on better promises.

> Because finding fault with them, He says: "Behold, the days are coming, says the LORD, when I will make a new covenant with the house of Israel and with the house of Judah...."

> In that He says, "A new covenant," He has made the first obsolete. Now what is becoming obsolete and growing old is ready to vanish away.
> (Hebrews 8:6,8,13 NKJV)

This New Covenant is the one by which the Church relates to God. The New Covenant is also the one the Church must follow in matters of forgiveness and pardon.

Too, when Christ came, He instituted a new system of justice, one that met sin not with law but with grace. New Covenant justice shares some similarities with Old Covenant justice. Under New Covenant justice, Christians must submit to the "commandment[s] of God" (Matthew 15:3 NKJV) or face consequences. Also, no allowance is made for personal retribution because, "'Vengeance is Mine, I will repay,' says the Lord" (Hebrews 10:30 NKJV). Further, desire for punishment cannot be generalized to include the innocent.

However, New Covenant justice is also different from Old Covenant justice. Under the New Covenant, penalties for offense are not set in cement as they were under the law; instead, each case is judged individually. Also, judgment is taken out of the hands of man and given to God. Perhaps the biggest change is in attitude. It was Jesus Himself who made a clear distinction between what was allowed in people's hearts under the Old Covenant and what He allowed under the New. Several times in Scripture, He recalled the past and then declared His own rule or authority for the present. Specifically concerning the issues of justice and retaliation, Jesus made a statement that cannot be ignored: *"You have heard that it was said, 'An eye for an eye and a tooth for a tooth.' But I tell you not to resist an evil person. But whoever slaps you on your right cheek, turn the other to him also"* (Matthew 5:38-39 NKJV).

He followed these words up with more of equally earth-shaking importance. *"You have heard that it was said, 'You shall love your neighbor and hate your enemy.' But I say to you, love your enemies, bless those who curse you, do good to those who hate you, and pray for those who spitefully use you and persecute you...."* (Matthew 5:43-44 NKJV).

In a few short sentences, Jesus revealed His heart. He slammed the door on vengeance and retaliation as a way of life. He absolutely prohibited any attitude or action of evil toward those who offend. Justice was no longer to be exercised according to Old Covenant law written on tablets of stone but according to the New Covenant law of love written in hearts. If punishment had to be meted out for offense, it would be meted out with the prayers and tears of the one offended, not with his or her hatred.

Thus, when the Old Covenant was changed to the New, our ideas concerning forgiveness and pardon should have changed too. Old Covenant lust for revenge and hoping the enemy got "all that was coming to him" should have yielded to mercy or hoping the enemy received less than he deserved. The Old Covenant desire of punishment for punishment, blood for blood, wound for wound, hurt for hurt, and offense for offense should have been canceled by New Testament grace. Even if offense ended with the need of discipline or punishment, it was to be assigned by God and accomplished in love.

OLD COVENANT AND NEW COVENANT JUDGES

We cannot leave the subject of justice without some reference to its judges. When Christ came and instituted a New Covenant and a new system of justice, He also changed the governors or the adjudicators of the law. The Old Covenant judge who was fallible and human was replaced by the New Covenant Judge who was infallible and holy. Though forgiveness was the responsibility of all under this covenant, judgment became the responsibility of God, the Judge of all (Hebrews 12:23).

In this authority, when offense is being judged, He can forgive sin and remove all guilt, condemnation, and death (Romans 8:1-2). Too, in this authority, He can fully pardon offenders, subject them to trial to prove their faith (1 Peter 1:6-7), discipline or chasten them (Hebrews 12:5-6), or refuse to pardon the temporal effects of sin.

When our holy Judge chooses to discipline or to refuse to pardon, He does not do so in order to hurt and to wound. Nor does He do so until we "pay for our sins." He does so to change our hearts so we won't willingly subject ourselves —or anyone else—to the pain our sin has caused again. He does so that we will be transformed, be able to refuse to indulge in choices of flesh, and be referred to as *"spirits of just men made perfect"* (Hebrews 12:23 NKJV).

There are several reasons why such a monumentally important task falls on the shoulders of our Lord. To name but a few:

1. Jesus shed His blood and died for the forgiveness of sin. He, more than any of us, knows the price He paid to make that forgiveness available to His Church.

2. When His blood was shed, it canceled the idea of blood for blood. His one-time-never-to-be-repeated, perfect sacrifice ended any future shedding of blood to forgive sin.

3. When Jesus went to the cross, shed His blood, and died, He forever changed the old order. No more would righteous Abel's blood cry out from the ground for vengeance. Now Jesus' blood would cry out for justice through forgiveness and love.

4. When Jesus rose from the dead, He became Mediator of the new and better covenant (Hebrews 8:6; 9:15). In all areas that are under the jurisdiction of the New Covenant—and for Christians that surely includes the realm of justice—He alone is the means of dealing with sin and of having right relationship with the Father.

5. Jesus is the Just One (Acts 7:52). He is fair, upright, and honest in all He does. He is impartial, true, pure, and honorable in executing justice. Since He was victorious over His passion in Gethsemane, He is not ruled by emotions; His judgments are impartial and objective. Since He is omniscient, He can rule wisely. Since He is the only Man without sin, He can judge in holiness.

6. When Jesus took on the form of a servant and was *"found in appearance as a man"* (Philippians 2:8 NKJV), He identified with us. Since He understands perfectly how it feels to be misjudged, since He knows what it is like to be wounded and betrayed, since He was subject to false accusation and unjust punishment, He has a heart for justice. Since He was badly treated at the hands of men, He will ensure that we can entrust ourselves into the hands of God.

We can only rejoice that we, who are under the New Covenant, have a Judge who can be trusted to rule impartially and justly whether we are the offender or the offended. Like Paul, who in a civil case could appeal to the highest human authority (Acts 25:10-12), in spiritual matters we can appeal to the highest Authority of all, the Judge whose decisions are absolute and cannot be overruled.

David must have had a revelation of such pure, holy judgment. He knew the terror of finding himself under the unholy, unfair, emotion-driven judgment of people. When he had sinned by taking a census, he confessed his sin and was offered three choices of punishment: seven years of famine, three months of pursuit by enemies, or three days of plague. Knowing whatever decision he made would bring calamity on all of Israel, he begged God to keep him free from the "justice" of man. *"And David said to Gad, 'I am in great distress. Please let us fall into the hand of the LORD, for His mercies are great; but do not let me fall in to the hand of man'"* (2 Samuel 24:14 NKJV).

We began part four of this book with some questions. We shall end this chapter in the same way. Concerning justice:

1. Do we understand that God has made important changes in His justice system that include both judgment and Judge?

2. Have we made the transition with Him from the Old Covenant to the New?

3. Are we seeking justice according to the law and people's legalisms rather than according to spirit and grace?

4. If we are the offenders in need of forgiveness, do we understand that if we use the technicalities of the law as our defense for sin and evil, we will be judged by the law?

5. If we are the offended, do we acknowledge that if we are seeking revenge and are demanding the full penalty of the law be assigned to the one who wounded us, we will fall under the same judgment?

We can't have it both ways! We choose either New Covenant or Old Covenant. We choose grace or legalism. We choose love or retaliation. We cannot claim the blessings of one for ourselves while seeking the wrath of the other for our neighbors.

Concerning the Judge:

1. Do we fully understand that judgment belongs to God, the Judge of the living and dead, who alone is the final authority over everyone (Acts 10:42)?

2. If we pervert justice by assuming the place of God and declaring judgment on our friends, co-workers, and Christian family, do we now realize the seriousness of our offense?

So, how do we forgive? Come under the New Covenant. Give up Old Covenant demands for justice. Leave everything in the very capable hands of God.

Chapter 16

PLACING VALUE ON THE OFFENDER

N o one said this was going to be easy!

Sometimes offense is light and leaves only surface or superficial wounds that are quickly and easily taken care of. Yet oftentimes, those who sin against us are in a close relationship with us and their words and actions hurt so deeply that resolution of them can be long and painful. In fact, when the severity of the offense is great enough and/or the perpetrator is someone we have admired, respected, trusted, liked, and prized relationship with, there can be all-out war in our souls before forgiveness wins over unforgiveness, bitterness, and continued animosity. Dealing with our emotions in a holy way and understanding the divine judicial system are two of our weapons in battle. Placing value on our enemy is a third.

Our journeys through forgiveness begin in some suspect places. After an offense (or repeated offenses), we may experience denial. *Surely that didn't happen....did it?* Next we may find ourselves bewildered. *How could he (or she) do that to me? We've been good friends. We've shared so much. How could this have happened?* Then comes anger. *I want to hurt him (or her) like he hurt me! I want him to pay!*

A big breakthrough in our struggle to forgive comes when we see these things as a normal part of our battle. An even bigger release comes when we realize that they are stepping stones in our search for peace.

Our journey through hurt, confusion, and tumultuous emotions produces actions and reactions that reveal truth. It shows us things about ourselves we may never have seen or admitted before. It is the measure of the state of our soul. When we realize that we are struggling emotionally and we realize that trying to establish justice through law is really an attempt to produce justice out of injustice, we recognize the first enemy we have to deal with is not someone else. It is our own flesh.

If we publicly or privately react to provocation with un-holy anger, we have to ask ourselves why we feel that this is allowable or appropriate. Or, if we publically or privately continue to demand payback for the harm done to us, we must cease hurling spears and shooting arrows at our antagonist long enough to question why we feel justified in treating him or her this way.

The answer to those questions lies in part in our assessment of value. If we do not value our offender, we allow ourselves any expression of wrath against him (or her). If we do not place worth, importance, or significance on our foe, we have mentally cleared the way for God to annihilate him. It is only as we find something in our offender to admire, appreciate, respect, or treasure that we will value him enough to win the battle and honestly forgive him.

So what is of value in our offender? Where is there any good in him (or her)? First and foremost, the answer lies in his relationship with God. He is loved and blessed by the Father, Son, and Holy Spirit.

Our offender is God's child. As our Father planned each of us before the foundation of the world (Ephesians 1:4), waited until our time had come, oversaw our conception and life in the womb, birthed us, and even now continues our maturing, so He did for the one we are calling our foe.

Too, Jesus died to secure forgiveness for the sins of everyone. This includes our sins—and those of our offender. If God valued our foe enough to send His Son to die for him (or her) and Jesus believed him important or worthwhile enough to sacrifice His life for, he is valuable in the eyes of God.

Further, if our offender has accepted Jesus as Savior and asked Him to be Lord of his (or her) life, then the Holy Spirit has indwelt him. If He has so esteemed and treasured him, so must we.

In addition to finding value in our offender through his (or her) relationship with the Godhead, it must also be found through his relationships with other people.

Each of us has been created in the image of God. Long ago in the Garden of Eden, God created Adam and Eve, and He then gave them a job to do (Genesis 2:7,15). He has used this same pattern for all of His human creatures to this very day. First, God brings us to life, and then He gives us the calling, training, and anointing for our life's work with Him. In other words, whether speaking of the natural or spiritual order, who we are and what we do are two separate but interrelated parts of our one being. Who we are is not what we do. Or, put another way, what we do does not define the inner essence of who we are.

To apply this insight to forgiveness, it is a great relief to know that our evaluation of a person's nature, character, and inner being need not be the same as our opinion of his (or her) behavior. If we are able to disconnect the person himself from his offensive activity, we can attach value to him even when there are legitimate reasons to object to his reprehensible behavior. Thus, if we can accept the person even if we reject his offensive behavior, we greatly increase our chances of honestly forgiving him.

In Chapter 14, we learned the sequence that our thoughts produce our feelings which produce our choices which produce our behaviors. This taught us that dealing with unholy expressions of emotions allows us to more easily make the determination of our will to forgive. Going back one step further in this progression, we can see that changing our thoughts about a person will change our feelings toward him. It is the catalyst that initiates the whole sequence of events, bringing even greater freedom in our choice to forgive. So, in order to bring needed change in our thoughts of our offender, we assign value to him.

Somewhere in our discipleship or our Christian walk, we should have learned that our value is not based on what other people think of us or do to us but rather on what God thinks of us and what Jesus has already done for us. The same applies to our offender. His (or her) value is not founded on our carnal, fleshly, angry assessment of him or of his behavior against us. His value is in God's assessment of his worth.

Therefore, if we pattern ourselves after God, we must refuse to dwell, meditate, or obsess over our offender's offenses against us and we must change our thoughts (ideas, reasonings, speculations, logic, analyses, and plots) concerning him (or her). Ultimately, this will change how we act or react toward him. If we place value on him or dwell on this changed perspective, we are on the road to forgiveness.

We cannot cancel the past. Things did happen. However, we don't need to dredge up bad memories, put them on spin cycle, and watch them come around and around and around again. If instead we assign value to our offender, that will change our thoughts of him (or her), our feelings about him, our choices concerning him, and our behavior toward him. In changing our minds, not only are we setting him free, but we are also freeing ourselves.

We are not done yet. Keep in mind that Biblically speaking, changing our minds means to repent. But isn't our offender the one who needs to repent? Yes, he (or she) is! However, perhaps he is not the only one. If we want him to repent of his unloving attitudes and behavior toward us, we must first repent or rethink ours toward him. If our thoughts do not include constant acknowledgment of God's assessment of significance and importance toward our offender from which comes our personal admission of his value and worth, our thoughts are hindering us. If our thoughts are hindering us, they are stifling or prohibiting forgiveness. We, not he, need to change.

Jeremiah was a prophet who was used mightily by God to declare that judgment was coming to the nation of Israel because of the people's idolatry and disobedience to God's Covenant. Due to this message, Jeremiah was subject to opposition, misery, and suffering. Coming before God one day in prayer, Jeremiah made a request of God: *"O LORD, You know; remember me and visit me, and take vengeance for me on my persecutors. In Your enduring patience, do not take me away. Know that for Your sake I have suffered rebuke"* (Jeremiah 15:15 NKJV). Going on with the conversation, he discussed with God both his calling as prophet and the difficulties and sacrifices that had come with the calling. Finally, his question to God was, If I have been so faithful, *"Why is my pain perpetual and my wound incurable[?]"* (Jeremiah 15:18 NKJV). In other words, why am I suffering in my relationships with the very people to whom you asked me to speak? Why is my relationship with You in distress?

God's response was quite pointed. Before He addressed the sins and actions of those who had come against Jeremiah, He spoke of the prophet's need of an attitude change: *"Therefore thus says the LORD: 'If **you** return, then I will bring **you** back; you shall stand before Me; if **you** take out the precious from the vile....'"* [emphasis added] (Jeremiah 15:19 NKJV). Then God eased the anguish of Jeremiah's heart with some promises. When he dealt with his own heart, Jeremiah would be brought into a place of quiet and safety and he would be God's minister: *".... you shall be as My mouth...."* (Jeremiah 15:19 NKJV). He would overcome the very people who had seemed like a bronze wall to him; they would fight against him but not prevail over him (Jeremiah 15:20).

God's word to Jeremiah is His word to us. When we are down and all but out because of the outrageous actions of those we once called friends, we must separate the precious from the vile. We must separate a person's being from what he (or she) has done and then attach value to him or see him as precious. When we have done that, things will change— for us. According to New Covenant instruction, if we meditate on *"....whatever things are true, whatever things are noble, whatever things are just, whatever things are pure, whatever things are lovely, whatever things are of good report, if there is any virtue and if there is anything praiseworthy"* (Philippians 4:8 NKJV), then the *"God of peace will be with...."* us (Philippians 4:9 NKJV).

Chapter 17

FROM THE HEART

The steps or phases of forgiveness come with divine guidance. Overshadowing all of them is one requirement of such supreme importance that it must be followed before, during, and even after the process of forgiveness is undertaken. This holy revelation is that true forgiveness is from the heart. Anything less, anything else is worthless. Underscoring the seriousness and urgency to incorporate love in the healing process of forgiveness, Jesus said: "*So My heavenly Father also will do to you if each of you, **from his heart**, does not forgive his brother his trespasses*" [emphasis added] (Matthew 18:35 NKJV).

Physically of course, our hearts are the main organs of life. Like pumps, they circulate blood throughout our bodies. They are so important that without them, there is no life. If our hearts stop beating, we die.

Yet the Scripture about our hearts in Matthew 18 does not refer to a physical organ in our outer or physical selves.

Rather, it speaks of our inner, non-physical selves, the very core of our beings.

In the New Testament, the word heart is the translation of the Greek word *kardia*, which means our deep inner being, our hidden inner being, or our real self. Our hearts are both the centers of our minds and thoughts (or our rational beings) and the centers of our desires, feelings, and passions (or our emotional beings). Added to that, our hearts are the spheres of God's influence on human life. They are the places where the Spirit of God resides in redeemed man (Galatians 4:6) and where Christ dwells within us (Ephesians 3:17).

Like our physical hearts, our deep inner hearts are the main "organs" of life in our inner beings. They are the seats of our lives and our strength. They are the peculiar internal and invisible combination of soul and spirit in each of us that forms our individual natures and defines our particular characters. From our hearts spring our external and visible personalities as revealed through our mental, emotional, moral, and divine words, choices, and actions.

Although this inner heart may be a deep, hidden place to a human observer, it is easily visible to God who *"looks at the heart"* (1 Samuel 16:7 NKJV). Therefore, God knows whether or not our outer expressions of thought and emotion and outward declarations of morality and right relationship with God match the inner reality. Since He has said, *"I, the LORD, search the heart, I test the mind, even to give every man according to his ways, according to the fruit of his doings"* (Jeremiah 17:10 NKJV), we must never act in any way that is a deliberate misrepresentation of the true condition of our hearts. On the

Day of Judgment, our rewards—or lack of them—depend on the state of our hearts.

Our hearts vary in condition. Some of us are very like Christ in our inner beings, and it is obvious in all we say and do. Others of us are not so mature and our hearts are less than holy. For instance, it is quite possible to have a hardened heart. In fact, Hebrews 3:7-19 warns us that the sins of rebellion and unbelief will lead us to be unteachable in mind and unruly in emotion and will cause us to disregard or to refuse to yield to the will of God. In the Old Covenant, Pharaoh is a perfect example of this. When repeatedly commanded to let God's people go, he would not listen to reason, refused the advice of his counselors (Exodus 10:7), and ignored the warnings of the first few plagues. The consequence: his hardened heart (Exodus 8:15) brought disaster on Egypt.

While evil conditions of heart can be produced by faulty thought processes, they can also be caused by uncontrolled passions and desires. A New Covenant example of this is seen in the man called Simon, the sorcerer. He had believed the gospel message and had been baptized (Acts 8:13). Yet when he saw that the Holy Spirit was being given to other believers through the laying on of Peter's and John's hands, he offered money so that he too might receive such power. Peter forcefully refused to indulge such covetousness, and he cited the condition of Simon's heart for doing so: *"But Peter said to him, 'Your money perish with you, because you thought that the gift of God could be purchased with money! You have neither part nor portion in this matter, for your heart is not right in the sight of God'"* (Acts 8:20-21 NKJV).

Since such hearts are not what God desires in His family, He long ago declared He would institute a covenant that would change hearts.

> *Behold, the days are coming, says the LORD, when I will make a new covenant with the house of Israel and with the house of Judah—not according to the covenant that I made with their fathers in the day that I took them by the hand to lead them out of the land of Egypt, My covenant which they broke, though I was a husband to them, says the LORD. But this is the covenant that I will make with the house of Israel after those days, says the LORD: I will put My law in their minds, and write it on their hearts; and I will be their God, and they shall be My people.* (Jeremiah 31:31-33 NKJV)

This covenant is sealed by the circumcision of individuals' hearts (Romans 2: 29). Thus, while it is still possible to choose a hardened, darkened heart, an alternative is available. In salvation, we become, *"a new creation"* (2 Corinthians 5:17 NKJV), and our spirits are quickened to new life. However, our souls, though sanctified, are still in need of change. It is only our Lord who can establish our *"hearts blameless in holiness before our God and Father...."* (1 Thessalonians 3:13 NKJV).

From this brief study of the heart, can we begin to understand the magnitude of what Jesus meant when He said that we must forgive *"from the heart?"* Since forgiveness is an internal attitude leading to external expression and since it involves the interrelated activities of mind, emotion, will, and spirit, it can only come from the heart.

THE HEART OF THE OFFENDER

The condition of forgiveness from the heart applies to both offender and offended. If we are the offender, it is evident that if there has been no change in our hearts toward the one we wounded, we aren't really engaged in the forgiveness process. Even if we say things that sound right and do things that look right, we are just going through empty motions. Even if we delude ourselves that such outward performances fulfill the letter of the law for forgiveness, we couldn't be more wrong. Such attitudes are not a search for forgiveness. They are pure hypocrisy.

Those of us who say one thing and mean another are hypocrites. Those who are insincere or who try to dissemble and deceive are imposters. Those whose words are double-talk, pretense, and sham are charlatans. When soft words are not a true reflection of a soft heart, beware!

In application, when, as offenders, we meet with God and have not changed our minds or attitudes about our sin, our hearts are hardened. This is not forgiveness. It is hypocrisy.

When we meet with the one we offended supposedly to seek his (or her) forgiveness, if we have not had a change of mind and a change of emotion that have led to the internal victory of spirit over flesh, this is not forgiveness. It is hypocrisy.

If we think one thing but speak forth another, or if we feel one way privately but hide our emotions and act a different way publicly, this is not forgiveness. It is hypocrisy.

If we do not enter the process of forgiveness with the sincere intention of admitting our guilt, repenting, confessing our sin, and asking to be forgiven, this is not forgiveness. It is hypocrisy.

If we go through a fake, forced performance, perhaps because of the coercion of religious hierarchy or the demands of loved ones or because we "just want to get it over with," this is not forgiveness. It is hypocrisy.

When any offender's plea for forgiveness begins with, "If I *might* have done something wrong" or "If you have *perceived* that I *might* have done something wrong" his or her heart has not been changed. There is no desire for forgiveness. This is hypocrisy.

Compare this to the candor of: "I did it. I was wrong. I'm sorry. Please forgive me."

THE HEART OF THE OFFENDED

Not all problems are on the side of the offender. The state of heart of the offended is important too. Unlike the above situations, when an offender sincerely seeks forgiveness, a sincere response is required. If we, as the offended, do not enter the process of forgiveness with the intention of forgiving from the heart, no forgiveness is possible.

However, if we have allowed God to change our minds so that we value our offender, this is not hypocrisy. It is forgiveness.

If we have come to the place where our emotions are balanced and we can *"Be angry and do not sin"* (Ephesians 4:26 NKJV), and if we have gained even a measure of victory over flesh, this is not hypocrisy. It is forgiveness.

If we are careful that the expression of thought and emotion are the same whether private or public, this is not hypocrisy. It is forgiveness.

If we refuse the pretense of faked, manipulative performance, refuse false affirmation by a still embittered heart, and refuse to be shamed into forgiving to meet human demand but instead choose the path of honesty and character, this is not hypocrisy. It is forgiveness.

Contrast the flippant, "Hey, no big deal! No problem! I didn't think a thing about it" with "Your offense wounded me deeply. I have had a problem with my attitude toward you. I am still struggling with my emotions. However, I do release you into the freedom of my forgiveness so we are both free to grow in the Lord."

This earnest admission of on-going struggle shows heart change is happening. Even if there needs to be further work, this sincere release is the essence of true forgiveness. When God looks into this heart, He will be glorified.

In the Bible, Jesus distinctly warned about hypocrites and their false ways: *"He answered and said to them, 'Well did Isaiah prophesy of you hypocrites, as it is written: "This people honors Me with their lips, but their heart is far from Me"'"* (Mark 7:6 NKJV).

Thank goodness, in our New Covenant we have Jesus within us whose Spirit changes our minds, passions, and desires. Only when He does so can we *"do the will of God from the heart"* (Ephesians 6:6 NKJV), and forgive.

Chapter 18

MULTIPLICATION

M any of us can remember long-ago days when we had to learn multiplication tables. In school or at home, with flash cards or without, using chalk and blackboard or pencil and paper, we drilled and drilled and drilled until we knew that while a numeral times a numeral equaled a lot, zero times zero equaled zero. Even then, nothing times nothing was still nothing.

Some of us would like to think those days are long over. Yet, if we are disciples of Christ, they are not. Applying our math skills in a different way, the Lord still asks us to multiply our forgiveness. If we do, each time we do, He multiplies our blessings.

We know that all sin requires accountability. On one hand, to be forgiven, an offender must be responsible for his sin by: 1) confessing it to God and asking for forgiveness; and 2) admitting his or her sin to the one he offended, repenting of it, confessing it, and asking to be forgiven. On the other hand, to be forgiving, the one offended must forgive from the heart. This response is his only divinely authorized action, his only sacrifice of obedience that is acceptable and pleasing to God.

This is the prescribed way to deal with one response to one sinner about one sin. However, does it suffice for more? Does it cover a greater need? For instance, what if the same person sins against us over and over again even after he (or she) has once been forgiven? Is there a way to forgive a multiplication of sin? Are we in a situation where we, like Peter, are now asking (Matthew 18:21 NKJV), *"Lord, how often shall my brother sin against me, and I forgive him?"*?

It is interesting to note that this portion of Scripture that deals with the issues of multiplied sin and forgiveness immediately precedes and actually introduces the parable of the merciless and unforgiving servant. Since this lesson was relevant to Jesus' early followers in their understanding of forgiveness, it is also relevant to us, His modern day disciples. Since neither His Word nor His intent has changed in 2000 years, His instruction to His first disciples is His instruction to us.

When Jesus walked on the earth, oral traditions had been added to the law that the Hebrews were trying to obey. As part of that oral tradition, the rabbis taught that it was a good and a gracious thing to be forbearing enough to forgive the same person for repeated sin up to three times. Therefore, when Peter asked his often quoted question, it was an indication that he was questioning or refusing the legalisms and authority of the commands of men and was trying to stretch to a better way. His suggestion of, *"Up to seven times?"* (Matthew 18:21 NLKV) must have seemed very liberal to him.

While his attitude and intent were right, his answer was wrong. When Jesus replied, *"I do not say to you, up to seven times, but up to seventy times seven"* (Matthew 18:22 NKJV), He was not suggesting a definite number. Rather, He was declaring that there should be no limit to the number of times His disciples were to forgive. If the conditions of repenting, confessing sin, and requesting forgiveness were met, His disciples were not and are not to measure mercy or figure forgiveness. We are not to be occupied with counting offense but in freeing from offense. We are always to forgive and to continue to forgive.

Isn't that license for further abuse? Won't that make us targets of ongoing evil and unchristlike behavior? If our offender knows ahead of time that we are required to forgive all of his (or her) sins against us, will anything stop his continued, or even flaunted, acts of aggression against us?

One answer to this dilemma involves the accountability of the offender. Though the offender knows we are required to forgive him (or her) for each offense, he also must understand that he is accountable to God for each offense. Each time he sins against us, he must meet with God, repent, confess, and ask for forgiveness. When God, who reads all hearts, knows the request is genuine (even if repeated a lot), He will forgive. However, if the offender is not sorry and purposefully continues to assault and to wound us, God will step in. He will refuse pardon and perhaps declare a time of chastening or punishment until the unrepentant one changes in heart and truly seeks forgiveness.

Further, the offender is accountable to the offended. As the sinning one has to seek God for forgiveness of each sin, so too he (or she) is required to seek out the one he offended to request personal forgiveness and release for each offense. If our brother knows that he can only be forgiven by humbling himself before the one he wounds each time he acts offensively, he won't continue his hurtful pattern of behavior for long. The pleasure of sin will not be worth the price and the pain of it. The lightness with which it has been undertaken or continued will become a burden of guilt too heavy to bear.

Another answer to the dilemma involves the attitude of both offender and offended. Sometimes an offender is not hostile or aggressive but repeats his (or her) sin because he is young and immature in things holy. He simply does not know the offense he is causing or the painful consequences of it. The offended, though, can constantly forgive their offenders while those offenders learn and grow in grace.

Occasionally, time has to be allowed while offenders learn not to become repeat offenders. In his wonderful book, *Intercessory Prayer*, Dutch Sheets leads the Church into a new understanding about repentance. For years, the disciples of God have been taught that repentance is a change of heart and a change of habit. Technically speaking, this is not wholly true. True repentance or *metanoia* is to have a change of mind or to gain a new knowledge or understanding. It is to perceive things differently and therefore to regret former actions committed under the old understanding. Then, as a fruit of repentance, comes a turning or a change, an *epistrepho*. This is to change direction or to turn and go another way. It is to change behavior or to turn from sin and toward God.

Generally speaking, repentance, or a change of mind about a specific offense, should precede forgiveness. Remember Jesus' directive: *"....if he repents, forgive him"* (Luke 17:3 NKJV). However, the process of turning or changing direction away from sin usually follows forgiveness since acquiring new habits and behavioral patterns takes time.

Between determination to change and victory in change there is often that awkward working-on-it phase where every bad intention seems permanently enthroned and every good intention ends in disaster. During this time, the offender confronts his (or her) character flaws and tries, by the strength of God and the leading of the Holy Spirit, to be rid of old, bad habits and to form new, good ones. During this time, those he hurt or offended can bless him by maintaining a posture that is kind and encouraging. If we are loving and patient while he puts *"off the old man with his deeds"* (Colossians 3:9 NKJV), if we are encouraging while he puts *"on the new man who is renewed in knowledge according to the image of Him who created him"* (Colossians 3.10 NKJV) and if we are *"bearing with one another, and forgiving one another"* (Colossians 3:13 NKJV), we are multiplying the effect of forgiveness on him—and on ourselves.

Can we see then that multiplication has a valid role in forgiveness? If the offender deliberately chooses to continue in his (or her) sin, there is no repentance, and therefore there is no forgiveness. Nothing times nothing equals nothing. If the offender denies or ignores his sin rather than confessing it, there is no forgiveness. Zero times zero equals zero.

However, if he (or she) sins and takes responsibility for the sin by earnestly following the path to forgiveness, he is forgiven and grows in grace. If his repeated sin is followed by honest, repeated repentance, his forgiveness is multiplied. If he is determined to change his behavior as well as his mind and his struggle, effort and humbleness are met with love, patience, and kindness by the one he hurt, blessings will multiply to an immeasurable amount—for both.

Biblically, the number seven symbolizes completion or perfection. When Jesus is exhorts us to multiply and to forgive *"seventy times seven,"* He is directing us to continue in forgiveness until it is complete. Even if it takes effort, even if it must be repeated over and over, we must continue until it is perfect.

If we feel that we don't have the strength equal to the challenge, we must remember that Jesus has never run out of mercy toward us. His mercies are new every morning (Lamentations 3:22-23). In addition, He has never refused any of our ongoing requests for forgiveness (1 John 1:9). In both cases, He is our example of our reaction toward those who have sinned against us. In our position in Christ, we can be merciful and forgive as He does—not just once, not three times, not seven times, or if you do the math, not even 490 times. As He forgives us our sins without limit, without measure, without boundary, so we must forgive those who sin against us—infinitely.

Mercy multiplied by forgiveness equals blessing.

Chapter 19

UNILATERAL FORGIVENESS

Until now, we have been learning that forgiveness is the interaction of two parties, offender and offended, which leads to freedom and release for both. However, such is not always the case. Sometimes the ideal is not the real. Sometimes when offense has occurred, only one person is willing to yield to the forgiveness process. Happily, even with such a regrettable circumstance, forgiveness is still possible. If two will not act together, if only one sincerely desires to reach the place of freedom, God offers the option of unilateral forgiveness.

Unilateral forgiveness is an attestation of the one-sided forgiveness that becomes necessary when there is rejection of joint accountability. It points to the non-reciprocal forgiveness needed if there is little or no hope that the 70 x 7 forgiveness process will ever take place on this earth as it should. Thus, unilateral forgiveness is the determination of either the offender or the offended personally to do all that meets the requirement for forgiveness no matter what the other does or doesn't do. It is the choice of one, not two, to act in obedience and faith, realizing that the completion of the process of forgiveness rests in the hands of God.

Several factors may lead to the breakdown of the forgiveness process. One of these is the unavailability of one of the persons involved. For example, the offender or offended may have died or may have moved away and left no means of contacting him or her. Or, one of them may be on his deathbed, so there is no time to go through the whole of the forgiveness process.

Another factor is the attitude of the offender. He (or she) could be in complete denial, steadfastly maintaining that his actions caused no harm, hypocritically pretending nothing happened, or flippantly declaring that what he has done was "for the good." Or, he may be irresponsible and simply seek to go on with the relationship that has been broken off without an apology, much less a confession of sin. Too, he may be convicted but be too proud and angry to yield to correction. He also may refuse guilt by projecting blame for the problem back on the one he offended. Finally, he may truly be ignorant of either his sin or of its consequences.

Likewise, the offended can hinder things too. He (or she) may not have successfully dealt with his thoughts, emotions, and will. He may be so deeply hurt that he is not able to forgive at that time. Or, he may be so shocked by who wounded him that he is not willing to forgive at that time.

Whatever the reason, all is not lost if one person is ready and willing to engage in forgiveness and the other is not. One person can unilaterally fulfill his (or her) personal requirements for forgiveness. Once he has done so, he can walk in freedom while the other remains bound.

In the New Testament, there are two outstanding examples of unilateral forgiveness. One concerns Stephen, the Church's first martyr (Acts 7). The other is the story of Christ.

The whole point of the cross was to secure forgiveness of sins. When Jesus was being crucified, it was visibly evident that He would suffer anything to gain this end. When Jesus was being crucified, it was audibly evident that forgiveness was His top priority. Bible scholars have written and preached on the seven sayings of Christ while he was on the cross. The first of these, indicating the importance He assigned to it, is *"Father, forgive them...."* (Luke 23:34 NKJV).

The account of Jesus's death by crucifixion reveals that there were many factors present that were hindering the process of forgiveness to the point that unilateral forgiveness was necessary.

First was the attitude of the offenders. Though both Jew and Gentile had conspired and plotted his death, both were in denial about their actions, hypocritically pretending nothing was happening, and surely thinking that their actions were a favor to their communities. Certainly they were irresponsible in their conduct and accountability even to the extent of projecting their own blame on Jesus or accusing Him for the problem (Luke 23). Without question they were proud and angry. Though they were pawns of Satan, Jesus declared that they were ignorant in their commission of offense. *"Father, forgive them, **for they know not what they do**"* [emphasis added] (Luke 23:34 NKJV). They didn't believe that they were murdering their Messiah, and they did not know the enormity of the consequences of His death.

Another factor that hindered engagement in the full process of forgiveness was the imminent death of Christ. Those responsible for His torture, agony, and death, that is Jews, Gentiles, and every one who had sinned (or who would ever sin), did not respond to the situation with repentance and confession of sin. There was no time or way for all to seek forgiveness. In fact, Jesus physically died before the process was even begun.

In spite of it all, there was forgiveness. If ever anyone who was offended had a "right" to withhold forgiveness, it was Jesus. If ever anyone had the chance to change the rules, it was Jesus. If ever anyone had reason to claim extenuating circumstances and forego forgiveness, it was Jesus. But He did not. Despite the circumstances, despite the decisions and actions of men, He forgave. He unilaterally forgave.

What Jesus endured could not have been more brutal or cruel. What Jesus suffered cannot be described or understood. Yet, His response to such evil and hatred was mind-boggling. After his betrayal and rejection, after His mock trials, after being scourged and beaten, after His death march through the streets of Jerusalem, after being stripped and whipped, after being nailed to a cross, after being hung aloft, He asked His Father to forgive his murderers.

His words did not release His tormentors from future accountability for their sin, but they did assure them that He held no ill will or resentment toward them. When He said they "do not know," He was not excusing their behavior from the requirements of justice or saying that nothing happened. However, He was keeping His own heart right with His Father.

In so doing, Jesus opened the door to future forgiveness. He made the way so that in days to come as awareness of sin set in, as hardened hearts softened, and as conviction brought repentance, there was yet a means by which they could be forgiven.

His example is for our instruction. There are two sides to every problem and both sides need to work things out. We are responsible only for our part.

Though pain and anguish may mark a particular season of life, none of us has ever come close to having to endure the things that Jesus endured. If He could seek the forgiveness of His offenders, so can we through the power of Christ who resides in us. It may take a while and it may be a unilateral decision and action, but it can happen.

If we are the only ones willing to engage in the forgiveness process, our first step is to confess any contrary attitude or action against our offender, ask for forgiveness, and make peace with God. It is from this position of peace that we can forgive others.

In no way does our unilateral action free our offender from responsibility. He (or she) is still accountable for each sin—but to God, not to us. He is still under judgment—but under God's, not ours.

This action frees us in every way. It keeps our hearts right with God. It keeps our hearts right with our offenders. It opens the door for future forgiveness. When our assailants are convicted of their sins, repent, and ask for forgiveness, they will not be blocked by our unforgiveness. In releasing them, we are released. In freeing them, we are set free.

Have we understood and accepted these truths? Forgiveness does not depend on circumstances. Forgiveness does not depend on other people. Forgiveness transcends both. Regardless of situation, regardless of the decisions of other people, forgiveness depends only on the command of God and our choice to obey it.

Romans 12:18 is an exhortation concerning our relationships with other people. It warns us those relationships won't always be perfect: *"If it is possible, as much as depends on you, live peaceably with all men"* (NKJV). If forgiveness is engaged in unto completion by both sides, God's requirements are fulfilled and the way is made for us to live in peace with one another. However, if that is not an option, we can still fulfill His requirement by unilateral action. At peace with Him, we can seek to live in peace with those around us. Like Jesus, we can expect our request for forgiveness to produce much—even if future—good fruit.

FORGIVENESS AND RESTORATIOIN

Also to be considered on the topic of unilateral forgiveness is the problem of the restoration of the offender and the one(s) he or she has offended. Ideally, when forgiveness is asked for, granted, and accepted, both parties will remain in relationship. However, at times the offense is so great or the relationship so broken that restoration, at least for a time, is not possible. Unilateral forgiveness may be followed by unilateral desire for restoration of relationship.

True friendships and meaningful relationships do not happen quickly. They are built over time; their main impetus is trust. When one person unintentionally betrays, offends, or wounds another, that trust is challenged. However, when one person purposefully betrays, intentionally offends, or deeply wounds another, that trust is broken. Even after forgiveness has been asked for and granted, reestablishment of the friendship or the relationship may not happen.

Restoration is not a requirement of forgiveness. Restoration is not a blessing that always automatically follows forgiveness. As the friendship or the relationship was first built through trust, so also a broken relationship can only be rebuilt through trust.

For instance, if a husband or wife has violated a marriage covenant, if a parent has abused a child, or if a person has been physically violent toward another, can there be a mending of relationship? Or, if betrayal has caused a business or means of livelihood to be destroyed, if the offense was marked by blatant disloyalty and deception, or if a wounding came from one who was so dearly loved that the pain was excruciatingly felt, can there be a mending of the relationship? Surely there can be forgiveness, but reestablishment of the relationship can happen only if both people who are involved in the situation want to reconcile and if the offender is willing to patiently rebuild the broken relationship by allowing changes in his (or her) mind, emotions, will, and actions that will prove him to be trustworthy over a period of time.

However, what if one of the people involved does not desire restoration of the relationship? What the offended no longer trusts the offender and has no wish to continue the friendship? What if the offender is so caught up in his (or her) sins that he does not care that he has wounded and betrayed the offended and, instead of seeking reconciliation and restoration, he decides to continue on his merry way? Then, temporarily at least, even as there is unilateral desire for forgiveness, there is unilateral desire for reconciliation. One of the persons involved in the situation must make his desire for reconciliation known and then leave the other person in the hands of God.

The good news is that Jesus has provided us with the gift of forgiveness. That gift includes the blessings of reconciliation and of restoration. Through His suffering and death, we are forgiven of our sins, reconciled with our Father, and restored to right relationship and intimate communion with Him. Through the ongoing power of His cross, those same blessings can change our natural situations from estrangement to peace. As we wait and pray, we can either forgive our offenders or ask that those we offended forgive us, we can be reconciled with rather than separated from them, and we can look forward to the restoration of deep and meaningful relationship with each other.

Chapter 20

IDENTIFYING WITH

THE CROSS OF CHRIST

For our hearts to be truly free of any resentment or ill will against anyone who has offended us, there is one more step on the path of forgiveness that is so profound, basic, necessary, and important that without it, deep, meaningful forgiveness is impossible. That is, we can forgive only as we understand and identify with the cross of Christ.

Forgiveness is the very heart or center of the cross. Forgiveness is the fruit of or reason for the cross. In the first century, Jesus sowed the seed of forgiveness at Calvary. In the twenty-first century, we are still reaping its blessings. True forgiveness, lasting forgiveness, victorious forgiveness, and necessary forgiveness are available from no other place.

All forgiveness is linked to Christ. It is specifically related to the cross of Christ (Acts 5:30-31). The purpose of the cross was for the forgiveness of debts (Matthew 6:12), of trespasses (Matthew 6:14), of sins (Luke 5:20) and even of the thoughts of the heart (Acts 8:22). Such forgiveness was no easy feat. It came at a very high price.

In His holiness, God our Father is loving, merciful, and gentle. He is also innocent, pure, just, and righteous. In His kingdom, no sin can be overlooked or ignored. Though it is our Father's nature to be forgiving and He truly wants to release those who sin against Him from the debt due for their offenses, He must balance mercy and longing for fellowship with judgment.

Long before this world was formed, God perfected a plan. He was going to create a race called humans. He foreknew that they would sin and, as a result, they would be separated from Him and lose their Spirit-to-spirit communion with Him. He decided that the only acceptable way for mankind to be forgiven of their sins, quickened from spiritual death into new life, and reinstated into right relationship with God was through sacrifice, blood, and death. *"For the wages of sin is death, but the gift of God is eternal life in Christ Jesus our Lord"* (Romans 6:23 NKJV).

Since He was *"the brightness of His glory and the express image of His person"* (Hebrews 1:3 NKJV), Jesus could be God's representative here on earth. God the Father sent His Son to propitiate or to satisfy holy wrath for sin. Through His sacrifice and death, Jesus could divert the wrath we deserved onto Himself so we could be forgiven and restored to right relationship with our Father.

Thus, when the time was right, Jesus gave up the splendors and acclaim of the courts of heaven and was born a babe, the son of a virgin named Mary, in a lowly animal shelter. As He grew to manhood, He *"increased in wisdom and stature, and in favor with God and men"* (Luke 2:52 NKJV). Since He remained completely sinless in all He thought, said, or did (2 Corinthians 5:21, Hebrews 4:15), He was the only Man who could offer Himself in the place of mankind as a pure, innocent sacrifice for man's sin.

Not while we were free but while we were slaves to sin, Jesus atoned for us. Not while we were innocent but when we were guilty, Jesus died for us. Not while we were alive in Christ but when we were dead in sin, Jesus gave us new life. Not while we were in right relationship with our Creator and Father but when we were estranged from Him, Jesus translated us into the family of God. Not when we deserved it but when we didn't, Jesus became our Substitute and paid the full price for our sin (Romans 6:23). In so doing, Jesus made provision for the full forgiveness of all sin.

On a day that outranks all others in human history for infamy, shame, dishonor, and wickedness, He was taken to a hill called Calvary and there, like a sin offering which was burned outside the city, He was sacrificed to provide the forgiveness of sin for the whole of mankind.

Without the shedding of blood there would be no remission of sin (Hebrews 9:22). Jesus was scourged, beaten, whipped, and punctured until His blood flowed freely. Under the Old Covenant, without the sacrifice of an innocent animal, there would be no forgiveness of sin. Under the New Covenant, Jesus was the sinless Lamb of God who was slaughtered.

When He had met all of God's requirements and had completed the provision for forgiveness, Jesus rose from the dead (2 Corinthians 5:15). God honored His suffering and sacrifice for the forgiveness of sins by receiving Him up into glory (1 Timothy 3:16).

While provision had been made for the forgiveness of all sins, forgiveness was not automatically granted. Since each of us has sinned, it is only as we realize our deep poverty in soul and death in spirit; only as we acknowledge that our sinful behavior has been offensive to God; only as we earnestly desire to be reconciled into right relationship with God through the forgiveness of our sins; and only as we individually approach the Father through the sacrifice of the Son, repent, confess our sins and ask to be released from the penalty due them that we are forgiven. Only by asking Jesus to save us from our sins—to be our Savior—are we set free.

This initial experience of forgiveness during our spiritual rebirth shows us the path or the way for all subsequent forgiveness when we sin again. Approaching the Father through the Son, repenting, confessing, and requesting forgiveness through the cleansing blood of the Lamb is the only way God will grant it.

Yet forgiveness is not meant to be a blessing only for us. God's grace abounds towards everyone. Jesus was the Sacrifice and the Substitute for all. As we believe in Him and cry out to Him, the blessing of forgiveness associated with our salvation or sanctification brings responsibility towards others. We who have been forgiven are obligated to forgive and Jesus has modeled the only acceptable manner of doing so.

Scripture clearly describes the high cost of discipleship: *"If anyone desires to come after Me, let him deny himself, and take up his cross daily, and follow Me"* (Luke 9:23 NKJV). Simply put, if we are to be Christ-like in our forgiveness, we have to deny our mind, emotions, and will any right for revenge; we have to sacrifice things that are dear to us; and we have to follow holy example.

Forgiveness is the only basis of our right relationship with God. He has forgiven us, the very ones who sinned against Him, by His sacrifice and death. Likewise, forgiveness is a cornerstone of our right relationships with our brothers and sisters in Christ. We must forgive the very ones whose wounds, attacks, and offenses have hurt us by our own sacrifices and death to self. As we were once reconciled to our Father through forgiveness so complete that He no longer looks on us with judgment so too, we are reconciled to our fellow saints through such heartfelt forgiveness that we no longer subject them to our judgment instead of our love.

In addition to revealing the cost of following Jesus, Scripture also reveals divine order to us: *"….the spiritual is not first, but the natural, and afterward the spiritual"* (1 Corinthians 15:46 NKJV).

Jesus was the Pioneer whose sacrifice brought forgiveness. He is our example or model. What He did in the natural world, we must do in the spiritual.

Too, Jesus was the Ambassador whose death reconciled us to God (Romans 5:9-11). He is our example and role model. What He did in the physical world, we must do in the spiritual.

Once in Christ, the job of Ambassador becomes ours (2 Corinthians 5:20). As such, we are commissioned to act on God's behalf to reconcile sinners in the world to Him (2 Corinthians 5:19). We are to bring the unsaved to and through salvation or to oversee their establishment into right relationship with God.

Additionally, once in Christ, we are commanded to engage in the process that will reconcile saints who are in strained, difficult circumstances with God and with other people. We are first to yield to God's testing and squeezing and to encourage other saints to submit to it until we are all returned to closer relationship with Him and to peace with each other (Matthew 18:15).

Whenever engaged in either job, whether sent to unsaved or saved, we can only fulfill our calling as ambassadors through forgiveness, and forgiveness comes only through the cross.

If all of this sounds impossible, we must remember the power of the blood of Jesus and the power of resurrection life. With God, all things are possible (Luke 1:37). It is true that we cannot do this on our own. However, no one is asking us to. Jesus has borne our griefs and has carried our sorrows (Isaiah 53:4). He is in us (Galatians 2:20), and His forgiveness is our strength.

To grasp our position of strength, we must understand that Jesus was not alone on His cross. He was in some awesome and powerful company since *"….God was in Christ reconciling the world to Himself, not imputing their trespasses to them…."* (2 Corinthians 5:19 NKJV). Rather than keeping a strained separation from heaven, rather than being an aloof or passive bystander, God the Father took an active part in the reconciliation process.

Too, Jesus was in some vastly less awesome and powerful but still greatly loved company, for we were with Him on the cross, as well. Romans 6:6 (NKJV) tells us, *"....our old man was crucified with Him...."* [emphasis added] and Romans 6:4 (NKJV) says, *"....we were buried with Him through baptism into death..."* [emphasis added]. All of this was for a specific reason: *"....that just as Christ was raised from the dead by the glory of the Father, even so we also should walk in newness of life"* (Romans 6:4 NKJV).

When forgiven of our sins, we become His disciples and members of His royal priesthood (1 Peter 2:9). As such, under the New Covenant we spiritually perform many of the same jobs that Levitical priests physically performed under the Old Covenant. We represent God to man and man to God. We reconcile man to God through instruction and presentation of the Good News that Jesus died for the forgiveness of sins. We reconcile people to people (or reconcile ourselves to others) through identifying with His death and through dying to self for the forgiveness of our offenders.

Too, we offer sacrifice. Like God when there has been offense, we must love enough to take the first step of reconciliation. Like Jesus, the sacrifice and death required may be our own. As God's holy priesthood, there are times when offering up our evil or carnal thoughts, reasonings, vain imaginations, idle speculations, feelings, emotions, passions, desires, dreams, plans, demands, commands, decisions, and contrary choices of will are the only *"spiritual sacrifices acceptable to God through Jesus Christ"* (1 Peter 2:5 NKJV).

To be successful priests, we need to go to the cross. We need to die to flesh and to self. We need to come to the place where we bleed for the position of the offender. No matter how hurtful, no matter how painful, no matter how long lasting, we must stay on the cross until we are dead to the wrong(s) done, crucified to all that is unholy, and willing to refuse all that is world-like rather than Christ-like in our reaction to offense. In so doing, we are preparing the way of forgiveness. We are made ready to discharge debt, release from resentment, free from obligation to us. We become changed so we can institute change.

This is not easy! Before Jesus went to the cross, He struggled with human thoughts, emotions, and will. He had every man's natural aversion to losing life, especially since He knew that in His case, it would be in such a brutal and agonizing way. However, after His struggle in Gethsemane, victory came. After a prolonged engagement with His inner man, He could say to His Father, *"....not My will but Yours, be done"* (Mark 14:36; Luke 22:42 NKJV).

So too with us. Sacrifice is not easy. When we have been deeply wounded, there will be a struggle before we can truly forgive. In our conflict, every fiend of darkness will whisper, "Why should you forgive? He's the one who hurt you." Every facet of flesh will rise up to nurse resentment and to speculate revenge. Yet after our warfare, if we do not yield to such unholy enticement, there is victory. We too come to the place where we say, "Dear Father, not my thoughts of evil. Not my judgment. Not my anger and fear. Not my desires to get even. Not my wish for payback or revenge. Not my will but Yours be done. Forgive them as you have forgiven me!"

When we have stayed on our cross and bled until we can't bleed to these wounds any longer, when we have remained on the altar long enough that all indignation and wrath has been burned up, when we have endured until God knows we are dead to the sin and the situation, we are raised to new life in which His Spirit brings about forgiveness, peace, and reconciliation. It may be unilateral, wherein our heart has changed toward our offenders but theirs have not changed toward us. Ideally however, if others have been brought through the same place of sacrifice, there will be unity, restoration, and forgiveness for all involved.

Make no mistake! Do not misunderstand! We are in no way equating or equalizing our sacrifice with that of Christ. He was innocent; we were guilty. He died in flesh; we die to flesh. He died once, perfectly; we die daily. He did all that was necessary for the forgiveness of all sin; we can only identify with His work, appropriate the strength and beauty of it and emulate it in our own need to be forgiven and to forgive. Yet as God sees our determination to yield to holiness and to obey His commands to do all we can do, even unto death, in order to bring freedom to the captives through our forgiveness, He will honor our sacrifice just as He did that of Jesus Christ.

When others have offended, we must die to all soulish inclinations. While their offenses are outstanding against them, we need to take the first step toward releasing them from our ill will by extending mercy. Then while they are dead in trespass and sin, we must lead them toward restoration. While they are out of right relationship, we must help them find their way back into fellowship with God, with us, and with others—all accomplished through our forgiveness.

Until now, we have been speaking of gaining or granting forgiveness through identifying with Christ and His cross, His sacrifice, and His blood. However, there is another option. Either we identify with the work of the cross for forgiveness or we disassociate ourselves from it. We accept Jesus' sacrifice for forgiveness or we reject it.

To deny the purpose of the cross is to deny the fruit of the cross. To deny the power of the cross is to make the cross of Christ to no avail.

This brings us to the place of decision. We can be forgiven through the sacrifice of Jesus Christ or not. We can be forgiving through the sacrifice of Jesus Christ or not.

Which do we choose?

Chapter 21

THE BIBLICAL PATHWAY
TO FORGIVENESS

In section four of this book we have been learning some of the "how-tos" of forgiveness. To review, we may have had to bring immature, unruly emotions into balance with our mind and will so they are no longer leading us into error. We may have had to realize that demands for retaliation and revenge that were right under the Old Covenant do not bring New Covenant justice. We may have determined to value an offender's being but not his behavior. We may have learned that forgiveness that is not from the heart is not forgiveness, or have been provoked to realize forgiveness must be multiplied unto perfection. Further, to our sorrow, we may now accept that sometimes forgiveness is a unilateral or one-sided act, rather than a dual act of forgiveness and restoration. Finally, we may now realize that our forgiving others is a reflection of the graciousness of God in forgiving us.

However, others of us may not have begun to consider any of these as a part of the forgiveness process. Even so, we must keep in mind that they are foundation stones, and all of us will have to deal with these issues sooner or later. We also must keep in mind that since each saint is different, since each offense is different, and each situation is different, God's timing for the resolution of offense in our lives will be different. While God works on these aspects of forgiveness within us according to our level of maturity and according to the timing of His plan for our lives, there are other steps to forgiveness that should be quickly applied to each incidence of offense.

Any time there is an attempt to introduce steps to accomplish a goal, there is a risk involved. Thus, amidst the instruction on the reasons why and the ways to forgive, there must be a disclaimer. The Old Covenant is a book of rite, outward performance, and strict obedience to law. Under it, if a person followed a particular procedure, he or she could gain a particular end. Not so today. *"But now we have been delivered from the law, having died to what we were held by, so that we should serve in the newness of the Spirit and not in the oldness of the letter"* (Romans 7:6 NKJV). Under the New Covenant, while there are no more laws to rigidly, formally, or dogmatically execute on our pathway to forgiveness, there are principles to choose to obey.

Since not all agree in fact or in act that the New Covenant has made the Old Covenant obsolete, there is genuine concern that any guidelines which reveal God's will concerning forgiveness will be reviewed as law and be outwardly, religiously, and mechanically obeyed according to the letter of the law rather than according to Spirit. If that happens, there is additional concern that those following the path of legalism will expect their outward performance to meet their required end rather than allowing their inward change of heart to satisfy God's desired end.

Therefore, let it be stated from the onset that the "how-tos" of forgiveness are not legalistic gimmicks which, once performed, automatically lead to the resolution of relational conflict. Forgiveness is not a matter of letter of the law but of Spirit. It is not a religious act but a loving attitude. It is not a required ritual but a choice of will. If we want forgiveness to be a reality, we don't go through legal motions; instead, we simply obey God.

Forgiveness doesn't just happen. For it to be successful, it must meet God's—not man's—conditions. Through His Word, He has clearly laid out His requirements for forgiveness. Under the Old Covenant, these included individual admission of sin, repentance, confession of sin, and the appropriate sacrifice to atone for sin. Only when these stipulations were fulfilled was right relationship with God restored.

The pathway of forgiveness under law gives glimpses of it under grace. Under the New Covenant, it is not just a religious experience commanded by God; it is a relational one. Still under God's authority, the same principle of admission, repentance, and confession of sin are involved. For forgiveness to be honest and complete, none of them can be ignored, put off, or omitted. Further, they are required of all Christians. There is no exclusion of young or old, rich or poor, male or female, learned or unlearned, leader or layman. While certain steps have to be acted upon, they are a bit different for offender and offended.

FOR THE ONE WHO HAS OFFENDED:

1. **Meet with God.** The vertical relationship with God is our most important one. Though sin seems aimed at human targets, in reality, all offense is against God. Since sin separates us from God, when we sin our primary obligation is to seek God for reconciliation. We must pray, admit our wrongdoing to Him, repent, confess our sin, and ask for mercy and forgiveness. Assured that He loves us and that He will grant us forgiveness, we should thank Him.

   Then there is the horizontal aspect of relationship. All who are in covenant with God are brothers and sisters in Christ. Since we are in family relationship, we are under the law of love. When we have offended a brother or sister, in essence we have strained the covenant. We are accountable to that brother or sister, and we are responsible to do our part in restoring right relationship with him or her.

2. **Admit the sin.** It is without question that any time we sin, God will reveal that offense to us for the purpose of convicting us. When He does, we must be honest above all else. If He calls an action sin, so should we. If He labels a reaction as an offense, so should we. If we do not, we are saying there is nothing to forgive. In essence, we have aborted the forgiveness process.

If we have committed offense, no amount of denial resolves anything, for God knows all things. He is aware of our breach in right behavior. Whether we disclaim any knowledge of or involvement in a problem, He holds us accountable to the truth.

Similarly, defiance solves nothing. In fact, it moves the situation away from rather than toward resolution. We are always responsible for our choices. Even if we are resistant to the truth concerning this one event or continue challenging, opposing, and being contemptuous of authority for the rest of our lives, we still will be accountable to God in the Day of Judgment. Consequences of wrongdoing are not permanently avoidable.

3. **Meet with the one we offended.** When we have acted in a way that has been harmful or has wounded another, we must humble ourselves and go to him. Though this step is often a very hard one for us, it is highly significant. In fact, it is so important that if we refuse to do it, our disobedience hinders our relationship with God. If we are worshiping God and remember our sin, we can't continue to talk with God. Instead, we must go and seek reconciliation with that other person. It is only after we have done so that we can come again before God. It is only after we have done so that we can offer Him a gift. Such is the command of Jesus Himself. (See Matthew 5:23-24 and 1 Samuel 15:22).

4. **Repent.** In this meeting with the one we have offended, we must make it clear that we are sorry for our action (Luke 17:3-4). To repent is to change our mind for our

past action, to regret it, and turn from it. In repenting, we should tell the one we hurt that we have thought things over and that we were wrong about what we once decided was appropriate or permissible behavior toward him or her. We should assure them that if we had a chance to do the same thing over again, we would not.

5. **Confess.** Apologies are not enough. Rather than producing forgiveness, they dilute or divert resolution of the problem. Confession is commanded (1 John 1:9). To confess is to agree with. As we previously admitted our sin to God, now we must do so to the one we hurt. We must acknowledge or profess that our words or actions were unacceptable and agree that the one we offended was right in objecting to them.

6. **Ask for forgiveness.** We must specifically ask to be forgiven of the sin that has brought such devastation. Following the injunction of Scripture, we must ask in order to receive (James 4:2). In asking for forgiveness, we are requesting that all resentment against us for our sins be given up, that any debt owed for them is canceled, and that we are freed from them.

7. **Respond.** If we are forgiven, as we once thanked God for forgiving us, so we may now thank the one we offended for his (or her) expression of grace. Through the blessing of Christ in him, we are released. However, if forgiveness is refused, we must remember that we have done our part, and the situation now becomes the dilemma of the other person. For whatever reason(s) forgiveness is not given, all must be placed in the hands of God.

8. **Make restitution.** If necessary, we must restore any-thing taken or lost to the best of our ability to do so. We must try to make good by offering the equivalent of the loss or by helping to recover or restore it. Such acts of love will seal the forgiveness.

FOR THE ONE WHO HAS BEEN OFFENDED:

If we are the ones who have unrighteously suffered at the hands of another, the situation changes a bit. When we are crushed by another's sin, there are things that we, not our offender, must do.

1. **Meet with God.** If our offender's primary responsibil-ity was to repair his or her relationship with God, ours is to maintain right relationship with Him. We must seek Him and see if there is anything in us that has re-sponded in an unchristlike way to unholy provocation. If there is, He must reveal it and we must repent of it, confess it, and ask His forgiveness for it. If there is not, we must seek Him for strength not to fall into sin, for the desire and willingness to be merciful and forgiving, and for the grace to walk after the Spirit rather than after the flesh.

2. **Admit.** We must acknowledge that sin has happened. Rather than deny it, ignore it, or brush it off as unim-portant, we must confirm it. In facing reality, we must determine how the sin has affected us and how to pro-ceed. It is here, in a preparatory phase, that we can deal with our intense thoughts and emotions and we can decide not to compound another's sin with one of our own.

Too, we must determine how the sin is affecting the offender. Knowing that sin is only dealt with when it has been forgiven by God, to deny its existence leaves it outstanding. To do nothing about it leaves it as a burden on the offending one. Even if we think we have been doing him (or her) a favor by not bringing up his offense to him, in reality we are postponing and lengthening the time he's out of right relationship with God. This is not an expression of love; it is lack of it.

3. **Confront or meet with our offender.** When we have been wounded, often our tendency is to get in a righteous huff and to wait indignantly for the one who sinned against us to "come to us to make things right." Such is pure pride and sin. According to Scripture, when there is offense, we must take the initiative. We must humble ourselves and arrange a meeting with our foe (Matthew 18:15).

4a. **Discuss.** We must talk to and not about the person. We must openly and honestly speak truth while revealing our thoughts and feelings. Perhaps the person is unaware of his (or her) offense so our words bring revelation. Perhaps he is all too well aware and has been avoiding or postponing coming to us. A meeting between the offender and the offended gives both sides a chance to bring the issue(s) into the open, to expose sin, and to lead to better things.

4b. **Rebuke.** If the offender is in denial, if he or she takes a defensive, hostile posture, or if there is outright refusal to own the sin or be responsible concerning it, there is one more step the offended is authorized to take (Luke 17:3). Presupposing that we have dealt with our emotions and that neither anger or fear will cause problems, we can, with calmness, honesty, and boldness confront without affront. That is, we can bear solemn witness or evaluate the situation. We can express disappointment in the other's behavior and state our desire that it is restrained in the future. We can reprove, reprimand, admonish, advise of fault, and warn of error, all with the intent of resolving the issue.

5. **Allow repentance.** Allow the offender a chance to respond, to present his (or her) point of view, or to express his thoughts and feelings. Discover if he has really rethought his actions and if he really regrets them.

6. **Allow confession of sin.** Listen carefully while the offender confesses—or agrees with you—that his (or her) actions were wrong and harmful. Hope to hear the words, "I was wrong. I'm sorry. Please forgive me."

7. **Respond to the request for forgiveness.** If the offender has repented and confessed his (or her) sin, there are no grounds to withhold forgiveness. Remember, his petition is not that we forgive his sin. That is God's job. Rather, his petition is that we forgive him or dismiss our animosity, cancel our account, and let him go or free him from any accountability to us (Luke 17:3-4).

If our offender refuses to ask for forgiveness, we must remember that we have done all we are required to do. The only option at this point is to release him into the hands of God. Like the unjust servant of Matthew 18, he may find himself under the judgment of the King or in jail in the hands of tormentors until he has faced and fulfilled the requirements of holy forgiveness. Meanwhile, we are free to get on with our lives.

8. **Pray with him and for him.** Pray that the estranged relationship can be restored. Pray that the mercy and forgiveness of God will be followed by pardon. Pray all of us will learn and grow and mature. Pray for God's blessings. This is fulfilling the law of love.

In all of this, let it be acknowledged that God has set conditions in His Word and if the conditions are not met, there is no forgiveness. Forgiveness requires both repentance and confession of sin.

"... .*if* he repents, forgive..." [emphasis added] (Luke 17:3 NKJV)

"*If* he confesses...." [emphasis added] (1 John 1:9 NKJV)

It was earlier said that forgiveness belongs to man and pardon belongs to God. That is true, but it is not the whole picture. In reality, man has two responsibilities in forgiveness: grant forgiveness and bless the offender.

The forgiveness process puts us all on trial. It reveals how everyone, offenders and offended, will act. It reveals choices. It offers a time of war and a time of peace. Peace can be found in blessing any who are or were our enemy. Blessing our enemy could be the witness that sets us apart from the world.

In its long history, the Church has been known to turn a blind eye on offenders and so further harm the ones who have been wounded. It does not have to be that way. By changing its attitudes and its practices in forgiving, the Church can become a healing place where the gospel of forgiveness is preached, the brokenhearted are healed, captives are delivered, the blind see, and the oppressed are set free (Luke 4:18).

PART 5

THE FRUIT OF

FORGIVENESS

Chapter 22

LOVE

Then one of the Pharisees asked Him to eat with him. And He went to the Pharisee's house, and sat down to eat. And behold, a woman in the city who was a sinner, when she knew that Jesus sat at the table in the Pharisee's house, brought an alabaster flask of fragrant oil, and stood at His feet behind Him, weeping; and she began to wash His feet with her tears, and wiped them with the hair of her head; and she kissed His feet and anointed them with the fragrant oil.

Now when the Pharisee who had invited Him saw this, he spoke to himself, saying, "This Man, if He were a prophet, would know who and what manner of woman this is who is touching Him, for she is a sinner."

And Jesus answered and said to him, "Simon, I have something to say to you."

So he said, "Teacher, say it."

"There was a certain creditor who had two debtors. One owed five hundred denarii, and the other fifty. And when they had nothing with which to repay, he freely forgave them both. Tell Me, therefore, which of them will love him more?"

Simon answered and said, "I suppose the one whom he forgave more."

And He said to him, "You have rightly judged." Then He turned to the woman and said to Simon, "Do you see this woman? I entered your house; you gave Me no water for My feet, but she has washed My feet with her tears and wiped them with the hair of her head. You gave Me no kiss, but this woman has not ceased to kiss My feet since the time I came in. You did not anoint my head with oil, but this woman has anointed My feet with fragrant oil. Therefore I say to you, her sins, which are many, are forgiven, for she loved much. But to whom little is forgiven, the same loves little."

Then He said to her, "Your sins are forgiven."

And those who sat at the table with Him began to say to themselves, "Who is this who even forgives sins?"

Then He said to the woman, "Your faith has saved you. Go in peace." (Luke 7:36-50 NKJV)

No discussion of forgiveness would be complete without a revelation of its intended result. Though release from shame and guilt and the blessings of peace and restoration accompany forgiveness, its richest fruit or the proof of its reality is love.

In these Scriptures from Luke 7, we are introduced to two people of striking and vivid contrast who teach us about forgiveness. One is a respectable, self-righteous Pharisee named Simon. The other is an unrespectable, humble, unnamed woman. They were on the extreme ends of the religious and social scales, for Simon was a strict religionist whose duty as a Pharisee was to keep himself separated from sin—and by extension, from sinners—while the woman was a sinner from the streets, someone the shallow, unloving Pharisee would go out of his way to avoid.

As we read, one day the Pharisee asked Jesus to dine with him. For whatever reason, perhaps out of curiosity, perhaps to discover who Jesus was for himself, perhaps to have a trophy guest, or perhaps to find a reason to condemn Him, he invited Jesus to his home. And Jesus had come.

However, after Jesus arrived, the Pharisee acted as if He were not even there. He ignored and insulted Him by his lack of hospitality. Refusing to offer even the most basic civility or the minimal standard of politeness that was a normal part of Middle-Eastern culture, he did not: 1) provide Jesus water to wash off the dust of travel; 2) provide Him with oil with which to anoint His head; or 3) greet Him with a kiss, which was a traditional greeting.

Meanwhile, *"a woman in the city"* who was a sinner, had learned that Jesus was to be a guest at the home of the Pharisee. She went as well, to esteem, honor, adore, and love Him.

The word used to describe this woman, "sinner," means one who wandered from the way or who missed the mark. However, here, it seems to mean more. Bible scholars and commentaries agree that this use of the word describes a particular kind of sinner. The woman was a harlot.

According to the *Word in Life Study Bible*, in this first century society, there were those considered to be upper class and those declared to be lower class. Those on the questionable margins of society included the blind, the lame, the unable, the handicapped, the sick, the demonized, or the rejected as well as those who were widows, orphans, destitute, or refugees. They got by as best they could by begging, stealing, providing menial labor, being sold into slavery, or becoming prostitutes.

Apparently, the woman had existed among these outcasts, fallen and desperate. Yet among these, she had been singularly blessed. Verse 47, which says her sins "are forgiven" indicates a past action. She had been forgiven of her sins.

It is highly unlikely that a Pharisee, a strict legalist, a proud, formal religionist, would have had anything to do with this woman. Yet, so eager was she to be in Jesus' presence, so desirous of pouring out her love upon Him, that though unbidden, unwanted, and uninvited, she came anyway. Somehow she gained admittance, found where Jesus was reclining at the table, positioned herself at His feet, and worshiped Him.

In direct contrast to Jesus' inhospitable host, she washed His feet with the water of her tears and toweled them dry with her hair. She kissed them to greet and adore Him. She anointed them with fragrant oil from an alabaster flask she had brought with her.

Such evident adoration and reverence was too much for the Pharisee. He was angry and disturbed at the woman's sincere and open demonstration of devotion. Worse, he was horrified that Jesus did not refuse such ministrations. In his mind, if religious leaders, such as himself, were to remain separate from sinners, Jesus should have too.

Speaking only to himself, the Pharisee judged and condemned both the woman and Jesus. His words show disgust for the woman: "....what manner of woman **this** is" [emphasis added] (Luke 7:39 NKJV). They also reveal deep-seated contempt for Jesus: "This man, **if** He were a prophet, would know...." [emphasis added] (Luke 7:39 NKJV). Finally, they declare how much he admired himself, thinking that he was above behaving as she did or responding as Jesus did.

Then, as now, Jesus knows our innermost thoughts and judges the words we speak in silence (Mark 4:22; Romans 2:16). He heard the Pharisee's unspoken thoughts. Calling him by name for the first time, He asked Simon for permission to speak. When granted, He told a parable.

At first glance, this parable has some similarities to the parable of settling the accounts found in Matthew 18. Debt had been accrued by two debtors. The amounts of the two debts were different; one was much greater that the other. Neither debtor could repay, yet both were freely and fully forgiven.

However, there were also some differences. Matthew 18 deals more with people's relationships with other people while Luke 7 deals more with people's relationships with their Lord. Matthew 18 details the consequences from failure to forgive while Luke 7 highlights the fruit or harvest of forgiveness: love.

There are also some obvious differences in the principles being taught in these two parables. In Matthew 18, Jesus teaches that all sin is debt owed to God. When we are in debt to sin, whether overwhelmingly so or "just a little," we can do nothing to repay that debt. No works, no self-effort, and no personal achievement will suffice. The unpayable debt can only be settled if the one to whom it is owed cancels it. Therefore, we are released from sin only by the forgiveness of God. Too, in Luke 7, Jesus shows that we do not love in order to be forgiven. Rather, we love because we have been forgiven.

In general, Pharisees wore their religion on their sleeves. Since they majored in the formal and the legal, they were shallow and external. They delighted in outward show. The Pharisee in Luke 7 was cut from this mold. He had no depth of character. Nothing reached his heart. In such a state, it would never have occurred to him that forgiveness was related to love.

So Jesus enlightened him. To emphasize this new aspect of forgiveness, Jesus directly connected it with love in His parable: *"And when they had nothing with which to repay, he freely **forgave** them both. Tell Me, therefore, which of them will **love** him more?"* [emphasis added] (Luke 7:42 NKJV).

When Simon answered correctly, *"I suppose the one whom he forgave more"* (Luke 7:43 NKJV), Jesus confirmed his response. He then proceeded to strip Simon of some of his self-righteousness.

Simon had already judged the woman a sinner (Luke 7:39). Indeed, she had been a sinner. She knew all too well the depth of the degradation in which she had been living and of which she was guilty. Yet, at some moment unrevealed in the verses, she had met the Lord and been forgiven of her past. Her debt of sin had been canceled. Being forgiven meant she had been born anew, cleansed, regenerated, healed, and brought into right relationship with God. She who had been forgiven much loved much. Love poured out from her in boldness, devotion, and worship.

Simon was a sinner too. The difference was that he had assigned himself the fifty denarii debt. He did not see himself a serious sinner, especially as compared to the woman of whom he was in such contempt. Since he couldn't admit the extent of his sin, he couldn't realize the depth of his forgiveness. Forgiven little, he loved little. This lack of love stopped a true flow of worship.

Simon had secretly questioned Jesus's ability to see the woman. Now Jesus openly questioned Simon's ability to see her. Can't we hear Him even now? "Simon, do you *see* this woman?" Pause. "*Do* you see her?" Pause. "Do you really *see her*?" Pause. "Do you see her as I see her? Do you see her as she is now or only as she was? Do you see her present or only her past? Do you see her selling her body as she once did or offering her body as a living sacrifice now? Why is her accumulated offense against Me, which I have now forgiven, so scandalous to you?"

Then Jesus revealed what He saw. Again, can't we hear Him? "I see a woman reborn. Her sins, which were many, are forgiven. I see a regenerated woman, a restored woman, a whole woman, a woman given new life. I see a free woman."

"I see a woman whose present ministry is love. She has done for Me all that you did not do because she loved Me."

"I see a woman pure of heart and pure of motives. She did not sell her love to gain forgiveness. She freely gave her love because she was forgiven. She didn't love to gain pardon. She loved because she was pardoned."

Liking what He saw in the woman's heart, Jesus reaffirmed her forgiveness and sent her away in peace.

What joy to know that God's words are eternal and His revelations everlasting! From this first century situation, there is twenty-first century application. From these first century people, there is twenty-first century encouragement.

THE INDIVIDUAL BLESSING OF FORGIVENESS

Concerning personal application, if we are honest, each of us can identify with one or both of the main characters found in the verses under discussion in Luke 7:36-50.

Perhaps we are similar to the Pharisee. Like Simon, we may once have asked Jesus to come into our homes or our hearts. However, since He responded to our invitation and came, we have been ignoring Him. We may be denying Him basic politeness and common civility and keeping our relationship with Him distant, formal, and minimal. Due to our failure to honor His presence, we are only dimly aware of how great He is and just barely grateful for all He has done for us.

If there is any Pharisee in us, our failure to properly relate to God is quite evident in our inability to lovingly worship Him. Refusal of deep personal relationship with God can only result in shallow, distant acquaintance as practiced in cold, dead, religious rites and observances. Refusal of close relationship can only lead to superficial, remote association as performed in perfected rituals and formal ceremonies. None of these come close to the richness of fellowship He desires.

If refusal of and denial of intimacy mark our relationship with God, they harm our relationship with others too. With them also we may only relate in shallow, external ways. Further, if we are blinded to the truth of our ignorance, coldness, and pride, we may begin to see ourselves as superior.

If we fail to compare ourselves with God in order to become aware of the vast differences between His beauty, perfection, character, and being and our own and instead choose to contrast ourselves with others whose sins may be well known or even notorious in order to make ourselves look good, we have entered the path of judgment. In continuously congratulating ourselves that we have never robbed a bank, killed anyone, committed adultery, or even that we are *"not like any other men"* (Luke 18:11 NKJV), we place them beneath us. We put them down, hold them in contempt, and label them losers.

We can identify with the Pharisee if: we see ourselves as superior and others as inferior, we judge ourselves as right and others as wrong, or we have a distorted image of our greatness and perfection and others' smallness and failure.

We can identify with the Pharisee if we have not allowed the Word of God to instruct us nor the Spirit of God to change us.

We can identify with Pharisee if we are so enamored of whom we think we are that we are blind to who we really are.

Long ago another Pharisee named Paul needed to have His eyes miraculously blinded and then spiritually opened before he could call himself the chief sinner (1 Timothy 1:15). If, in our Phariseeism, we don't have a similar revelation, we won't think of ourselves as serious sinners, we won't know the depravity of sin, and we won't know the cost of our salvation and forgiveness. As a result, we won't be able to deeply love.

Or, perhaps we see ourselves more like the woman. Not all harlotry is limited to ungodly sexual involvement. When reborn spiritually, even harlotry has a spiritual aspect.

In the kingdom of God, as in the world, harlotry is selling ourselves to loose moral living. Harlotry is anything that we give ourselves to that is unholy or wrong for us. Harlotry is gaining things by means that break our purity with God. Harlotry is seeking or allowing ungodly yoking. Harlotry is giving ourselves to wrong or illegitimate authority over us. Harlotry is dalliance with people in order to get what we want or need. Harlotry is unhealthy union in friendships and relationships that leads to unholy events, situations, and circumstances. Harlotry is prostituting ourselves to possess dreams, ambitions, positions, titles, jobs, glory, security, or material gain.

Harlotry is offering what we should not, accepting what we should not, or letting others take what they should not. It is unholiness in our souls. If any of these things mark our walk with the Lord, we, to some degree, have a spirit of harlotry.

Strange as it may seem, our Bibles indicate that it is more difficult for the smug, self-righteous Pharisee to learn to love than it is for the lowly harlot. The Pharisee had little awareness of his personal poverty, while the woman was only too well aware of the depth of her depravity and wantonness. If we can identify with either of these, we can know that forgiveness is ours through Jesus Christ. Forgiveness breaks us free from our narrow, restricted forms of religion and from the condemnation of our past to produce in us a very sweet fruit. Forgiveness makes possible the desire to and the ability to love our Savior.

We must find the One who forgave us. We who have been reborn, regenerated, and renewed to eternal life must go to Him. In spite of the hostility, disdain, and rejection of others (including the Pharisee within), we must boldly find our way into His presence. Once there, we must choose Him over all others and station ourselves near Him. Then, it is the highest privilege to cast ourselves down at His feet to cling to Him. It is the greatest blessing to wash Him with tears of joy, smother Him with kisses of delight, and anoint Him with the oil of our gladness (Psalm 45:7). It is our crowning honor to worship Him, extending back to Him the love that was poured out in our hearts by the Holy Spirit (Romans 5:5) at the time of our salvation. We love Him because He first loved us (1 John 4:19).

Whether or not we identify with Pharisee or harlot, we do identify with the debtors in the parable. Sin is sin. All sin requires forgiveness. When we have met the biblical requirements of repenting, confessing, and requesting cancellation of debt, sin is forgiven. Though some have fewer sins than others, all sin is forgiven to its deepest depth.

We are blessed with the quantity of forgiveness, and we are blessed with the quality of it. God's forgiveness is impartial. He has provided the same blessing for all. Further, it is transforming. As we realize and appropriate His provision of cleansing through the blood of Jesus Christ, we are changed. It is empowering. As forgiven new creatures in Christ, we are able to love Him and to love other people.

If those with a Pharisee spirit reject us, judge us, see us as unworthy, or hold us in contempt and disdain, we can love them as we are being held in the arms of our Lord.

Like the woman in the parable, we will not return to our old ways or repeat our past sins because the price is too high. Instead of living by the desires of our flesh or by selling our souls, we will live by the fruit of the Spirit. Forgiven much, we will love our Lord much.

THE CORPORATE BLESSING OF FORGIVENESS

Forgiveness is not solely concerned with individual saints. It is also a corporate blessing which requires a corporate response.

All who are reborn become members of the sacred assembly called the Church. The Church is the sum of its saints. The Church reflects the character and nature of all its saints. It is God's intent that His Church be *"a glorious Church, not having spot or wrinkle or any such thing, but that she should be holy and without blemish"* (Ephesians 5:27 NKJV). Such purity and holiness is possible only by a continuous sanctification process. Just as the cleansing for one comes through forgiveness, so too the cleansing for many comes through forgiveness.

One way for the Church to yield to cleansing unto forgiveness is to ask God to search our collective heart for sin. Since we know our individual weaknesses, which may include Phariseeism and harlotry, it is wise to learn whether or not they are corporate problems too.

There is no question that a Pharisaic spirit affects the Church. Long ago the Lord revealed that such an unholy, unchristlike legacy would dominate the end times Church.

> And to the angel of the church of the Laodiceans write, "These things says the Amen, the Faithful and True Witness, the Beginning of the creation of God: 'I know your works, that you are neither cold nor hot. I could wish you were cold or hot. So then, because you are lukewarm, and neither cold nor hot, I will vomit you out of My mouth. Because you say, "I am rich, have become wealthy, and have need of nothing"—and do not know that you are wretched, miserable, poor, blind and naked—I counsel you to buy from Me gold refined in the fire, that you may be rich; and white garments, that you may be clothed, that the shame of your nakedness may not be revealed; and anoint your eyes with eye salve, that you may see. As many as I love, I rebuke and chasten. Therefore be zealous and repent. Behold, I stand at the door and knock. If anyone hears My voice and opens the door, I will come in to him and dine with him, and he with Me. To him who overcomes I will grant to sit with Me on My throne, as I also overcame and sat down with My Father on His throne. 'He who has an ear, let him hear what the Spirit says to the churches.'" (Revelations 3:14-22 NKJV)

If we as a Church are tepid, if we are neither hot nor cold in our relationship with God, if we have no heart or joy through Christ, and if we are satisfied with outward rite and rigid ritual rather than personal relationship with God, then there is a Pharisaic spirit in our midst.

If we as a Church have become smug, independent, and self-righteous, if we are blind to our position and our need, if we are unwilling to see and unable to deal with corporate sin, then there is a Pharisaic spirit in our midst.

If we major in external appearance and minor in internal transformation, then there is a Pharisaic spirit in our midst.

If we fail to compare ourselves with God so that He could reveal our weaknesses and the things He wants to change in us and instead compare ourselves with the world and ignore or judge those lost in sin, there is a Pharisaic spirit in our midst.

If we compare ourselves with other parts of the Church and sneer at their struggles to overcome sin, there is a Pharisaic spirit in our midst.

If we, as the Church, can confess our sin of Phariseeism, then there is great hope. If we accept our need of holy riches, clothing for our nakedness, and salve to heal our blind eyes, we need to seek Jesus. When we call out to Him, He hears our prayers and our hearts' desires. When we invite Him, He will approach. Even now He stands at the door knocking. If we admit Him, He will come in to dine (Revelations 3:20). Once He is with us, we should follow the example of the woman and not the example of the Pharisee in order to love and to worship Him.

As the Lord has revealed a Pharisaic spirit in the Church, so He also reveals a harlotrous spirit.

Another name for the Church is the bride of Christ. What greater contrast can there be than that of an unclean harlot and a pure bride? One is a licentious woman selling herself; the other an engaged woman saving herself. One is a fallen woman giving herself to any man; the other is a pure woman restricting her passion for one (in the case of the Church, one Man). One is a morally depraved woman sleeping around; the other is a morally upright woman eagerly awaiting the coming of her Groom. One is a desperate woman searching for love in many men; the other is a betrothed woman growing in love for one Man. One is a lewd woman using men and being used by them; the other is a lovely woman who honors and is honored by a Man.

Would any man want to marry a bride whose only goal was to use him for her personal advantage or gain? Would any man long for a bride whose eyes were firmly fixed on his wallet and not on his heart? Would any man be satisfied with a bride who has tried to earn his favor—and that of many others—with her body?

The answer is a resounding "No." So, then would *the* Man, Jesus, desire a bride like this?

The truth is that the Church has been the harlot. Every saint in her has been guilty of but forgiven of gross sin and evil. Yet there's a greater truth. We, the bruised, bleeding, broken, and fallen have been so regenerated, renewed, and cleansed by the blessing of God that we are no longer considered harlots. Our transformations have been so radical that we are now the betrothed of the Son of God.

Though saved, the Church continues to undergo progressive sanctification. Since a past weakness was harlotry, as she prepares for marriage she must examine her present heart to ensure no traces of it have reestablished themselves.

If some people came into the Church in order to avoid going to hell rather than for love of God, a harlotrous spirit is in evidence. If some were saved in order to be healed or to be delivered or to gain a particular kingdom gift, a harlotrous spirit is in evidence. If some were born again in order to use God to fulfill their own dreams, goals, and ambitions or to use Him to build their own kingdoms, a harlotrous spirit is in evidence. If some came into the Church in order to sell fleshly favors in exchange for title or position, a harlotrous spirit is in evidence. If some joined the Church thinking they would give God a try, and if He didn't work out, they would try other denominations or religions until they could have what they wanted, a harlotrous spirit is in evidence. If some claim to be Christian but they cannot clearly distinguish the one true God from false deities, created gods, men, or objects that are idolized, they are not part of the true bride of Christ. Harlotry is in evidence.

As the spots and wrinkles are removed from the Church, as the spirit of Phariseeism and the spirit of harlotry is confessed and forgiven, the bride is rising. Forgiveness is releasing her growing love. She is turning her eyes on the Lord alone. She singularly desires only Him. Her growing awareness of the depth of her forgiveness is enabling her to more deeply love her Groom.

The greatest command ever given to Israel is the Shema: *"Hear, O Israel: The LORD our God, the LORD is one! You shall love the LORD your God with all your heart, with all your soul, and with all your strength"* (Deuteronomy 6:4-5 NKJV).

This command has never been canceled or changed. In the New Testament, it is confirmed by Jesus to be the *"great commandment in the law"* (Matthew 22:36 NKJV): *"You shall love the LORD your God with all your heart, with all your soul, and with all your mind"* (Matthew 22:37 NKJV).

The Church can only obey this command to love because she has been forgiven. In the fullest sense, Jesus loved and then forgave. We, on the other hand, are forgiven and then love. When we are forgiven, we can love our God with our whole being. When we understand the depth of His blessing and when love becomes our most internal and eternal hallmark, we will truly be the bride of Christ, and the Father will release His beloved Son to come for us.

Forgiveness and its fruit, love, will be the cause and effect of the greatest love story ever told.

Forgiveness and love were the focus of the banquet described in Luke 7. The Lord's desire that we open the doors of our hearts to Him so that He can come in to dine with us is declared in Revelations 3:20. When we, His betrothed, are without spot and wrinkle, there is the promise of yet one more grand and glorious feast with Jesus.

Forgiveness will engrave the invitation to the most glorious banquet of all. At long last, love will be brought to perfection when bride and Groom unite to celebrate the marriage supper of the Lamb.

www.ingramcontent.com/pod-product-compliance
Lightning Source LLC
Chambersburg PA
CBHW051949090426
42741CB00008B/1321